THE DEAL DECADE
Handbook

THE DEAL DECADE Handbook

Margaret M. Blair and Girish Uppal

The Brookings Institution
Washington, D.C.

Library of Congress Cataloging-in-Publication Data

Blair, Margaret M., 1950–
The deal decade handbook / Margaret M. Blair, Girish Uppal.
p. cm
Includes bibliographical references
ISBN 0-8157-0943-9 (pa)
1. Consolidation and merger of corporations—United States—Finance. 2. Consolidation and merger of corporations—United States—Management I. Uppal, Girish. II. Title.
HG4028.M4B58 1993 93-18026
658. 1'6—dc20 CIP

9 8 7 6 5 4 3 2 1

The paper used in this publication meets the minimum requirements of the American National Standard for Information Sciences—Permanence of paper for Printed Library Materials, ANSI Z39.48-1984

Acknowledgements

The tables and charts in this handbook were prepared from information collected and assembled at Brookings over a period of several years. We would like to thank a number of people who helped us out along the way. Barrie A. Wigmore and Martin Fridson contributed some of the raw data used to develop tables in Section II. Mark Roe, Steve Wallman, and the American Society of Corporate Secretaries contributed information used in tables in Section III. Martha Schary, Sarah Lane, Bronwyn Hall, and Tim Ruefli contributed information to the data used in the tables of Section IV. Data used throughout this book were developed with the help of an able team of research assistants: Sameer Ramchandani, Marc Rysman, Nam Pham, Alec Ryrie, Hensley Evans, and Gary Baierl. Irene Coray and Carole Hingleton provided secretarial assistance in preparing all the tables and assembling the manuscript. Jim Schneider edited the work and Susan Woollen typeset it.

Contents

1. Introduction

The 1980s were a particularly tumultuous time for U.S. corporations. More companies were acquired, taken private through buyouts, and restructured financially than in any ten-year period since the end of World War II. Billions of dollars were raised to finance these deals through the issuance of complex new financial instruments, some of which were called debt but had risk and return characteristics that made them resemble equity. Some old conglomerates were dismantled, but new corporate empires emerged.

What did it all mean? The reconfiguration of the corporate sector made huge fortunes for the dealmakers and the financial whiz kids who backed them. But the windfalls came at a time when many U.S. firms were losing their market shares to foreign companies and other firms were cutting back their operations and laying off employees. The causes and economic implications of the corporate restructuring transactions of the 1980s are analyzed in Margaret M. Blair, ed., *The Deal Decade: What Takeovers and Leveraged Buyouts Mean for Corporate Governance* (Brookings, 1993). In this companion handbook, we present summary statistics and details on that episode in U.S. corporate history.

By special arrangement with Automatic Data Processing, Inc. (ADP) of New York, Brookings was given access to data for 1979–89 in the M&A Database (the M&A Database is now owned by Securities Data Co.). This is a comprehensive commercial data base that tracks merger, acquisition, and buyout transactions. In section 2 of this handbook we present summary information tracking private buyouts that we developed from these data. We also summarize data from other sources on junk bond issuances and on aggregate changes in corporate debt.

The deals of the 1980s occurred in the context of changing ownership of corporate equities and increasing activism of shareholders. The controversies surrounding the deals themselves also led to alterations in the laws governing the control of corporations. Section 3 presents data that summarizes some of these changes.

Section 4 compares key features of the 1980s merger wave to those of the 1960s merger wave. Data on mergers from the large 1980s data base used in section 2 were spliced to an historical merger file developed at Brookings, which tracks merger and acquisition transactions from 1955 to 1979.

Together, the data assembled for this handbook provide some measures of the scope and complexity of the corporate restructuring of the 1980s. It may be years before the consequences of this decade of dealmaking can be fully understood, but the data assembled here provide a basis for further analysis of the period and its implications for the growth and stability of the U.S. economy.

2. Changing Indebtedness of the Corporate Sector

Debt-to-Asset Ratios

Critics of the mergers, takeovers, leveraged buyouts, recapitalizations, and other transactions of the 1980s argued that they harmed the U.S. economy because they helped drive debt ratios in the corporate sector to unprecedented and dangerous highs. From 1980 to 1990, total corporate debt increased by more than 150 percent to $3,369 billion, according to the Federal Reserve Board. But the effect of this new debt on the aggregate debt-to-asset ratio of corporations depends on how corporate assets are measured.

The top panel of figure 2-1 shows two measures of the debt-to-asset ratio for the nonfinancial corporate sector. In both, debt and assets are measured at book value. The Federal Reserve Board series measures debt and assets for both public and private corporations; the Compustat series has been compiled from data on publicly traded nonfinancial firms. Both series show a fairly dramatic increase in the ratio during the 1980s, but in the Federal Reserve series this increase follows a period of decline in the early 1970s. Although the Federal Reserve ratios are lower throughout than those in the Compustat series, they rise more steeply in the 1980s, in part because they include data for firms that went private in highly leveraged transactions. Most such firms were dropped from the Compustat data base when they went private. The Federal Reserve series reaches new highs at the end of the 1980s, but it is not dramatically higher than it had been during the recession of the early 1970s. The Compustat series rises throughout both decades and ends the period at around 65 percent.

In the lower panel, the market value of equity rather than the book value is used to compute the debt-to-asset ratio of the nonfinancial corporate sector. Again, the Federal Reserve series includes public and private companies, while the Compustat series is compiled only from data on public companies. When equity is measured at market value, the leverage of the corporate sector does not increase significantly in the 1980s. This measure is an extremely volatile one because it is driven primarily by movements in the stock market. The large runup of debt in 1972–74, for example, was caused by the collapse of the stock market rather than by an explicit effort of corporate managers to add debt to their balance sheets. In the 1980s a rapidly rising stock market counteracted the effect of the rapid expansion in debt on the ratio of debt to market value.

Source Notes, Figure 2-1

The Federal Reserve series came from "Balance Sheet of Nonfinancial Corporate Business, Excluding Farms," table B.104, in Board of the Governors of the Federal Reserve, *Balance Sheets for the U.S. Economy, 1960–91*, pub. C.9 (September 1992). The book value series is the ratio of total liabilities to total assets at historic cost; the market value series is the ratio of total liabilities to the sum of total liabilities and market value of equities. The Compustat series was compiled at Brookings from data on publicly traded companies in the August 1991 edition of the CD-ROM version of Compustat. All financial firms (those with SIC codes 6000–6999) were eliminated from the file for this calculation.

For the book value series, the sample was limited to companies that have valid data for both total assets (Compustat variable *AT*) and total liabilities (Compustat variable *LT*). The series was constructed by summing liabilities for all firms in the sample in each year and dividing by the total assets for all firms in the sample in that year.

For the market value series the sample was limited to companies that had valid data for total assets, total liabilities, and market value of equity (*MKVALF*). This series was constructed by taking the ratio for each year of total liabilities to the sum of total liabilities, total market value of equity, and total value of preferred stock (*PREFSTK*).

See Ben S. Bernanke, John Y. Campbell, and Toni M. Whited, "U.S.Corporate Leverage: Developments in 1987 and 1988," *Brookings Papers on Economic Activity, 1: 1990*, pp. 255–78, for a discussion of corporate leverage ratios using estimates of the market value of both debt and equity.

Figure 2-1. Debt-to-Assets Ratios of the Nonfinancial Corporate Sector, 1971–90

Book value

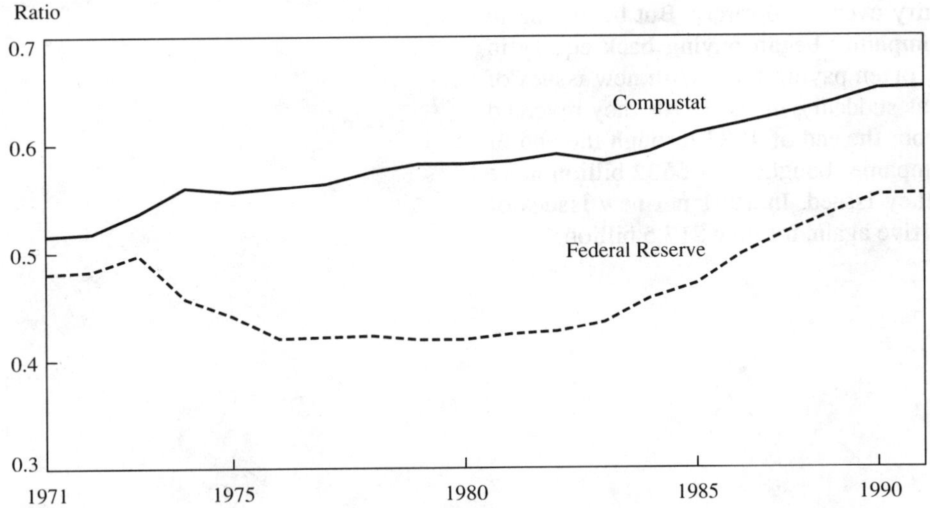

Market value

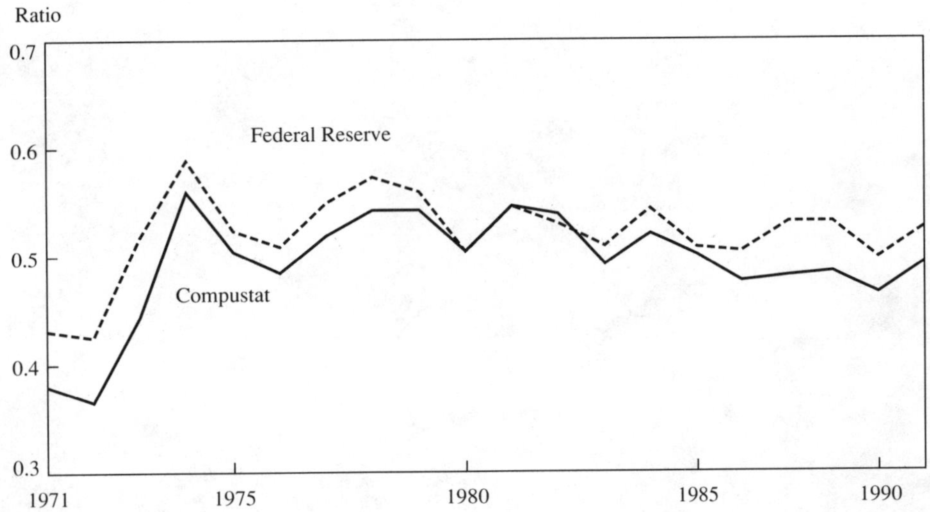

New Debt and New Equity

Changes in the patterns of marginal financing behavior in the 1980s were much more dramatic than aggregate changes in leverage. Figure 2-2 plots the dollar volume of net new equity and net new debt issued by non-financial corporations. Before the 1980s, corporations typically financed new projects using internally generated funds first and then using borrowed money. They rarely issued new equity, and they retired equity even more rarely. But beginning in 1984, public companies began buying back equity in record amounts, often paying for it with new issues of debt. Then just as suddenly, in the 1990s they reversed this practice. From the end of 1983 through the end of 1990, public companies bought back $632 billion more in equity than they issued. In 1991 net new issues of equity were positive again, totaling $17.5 billion.

Source Notes, Figure 2-2

Data for net new issues of debt and equity for the nonfinancial corporate sector come from *Federal Reserve Bulletin*, various issues, table 1.57 ("Funds Raised in U.S. Capital Markets").

Figure 2-2. Net New Issues of Debt and Equity, Nonfinancial Corporate Sector, 1971–91

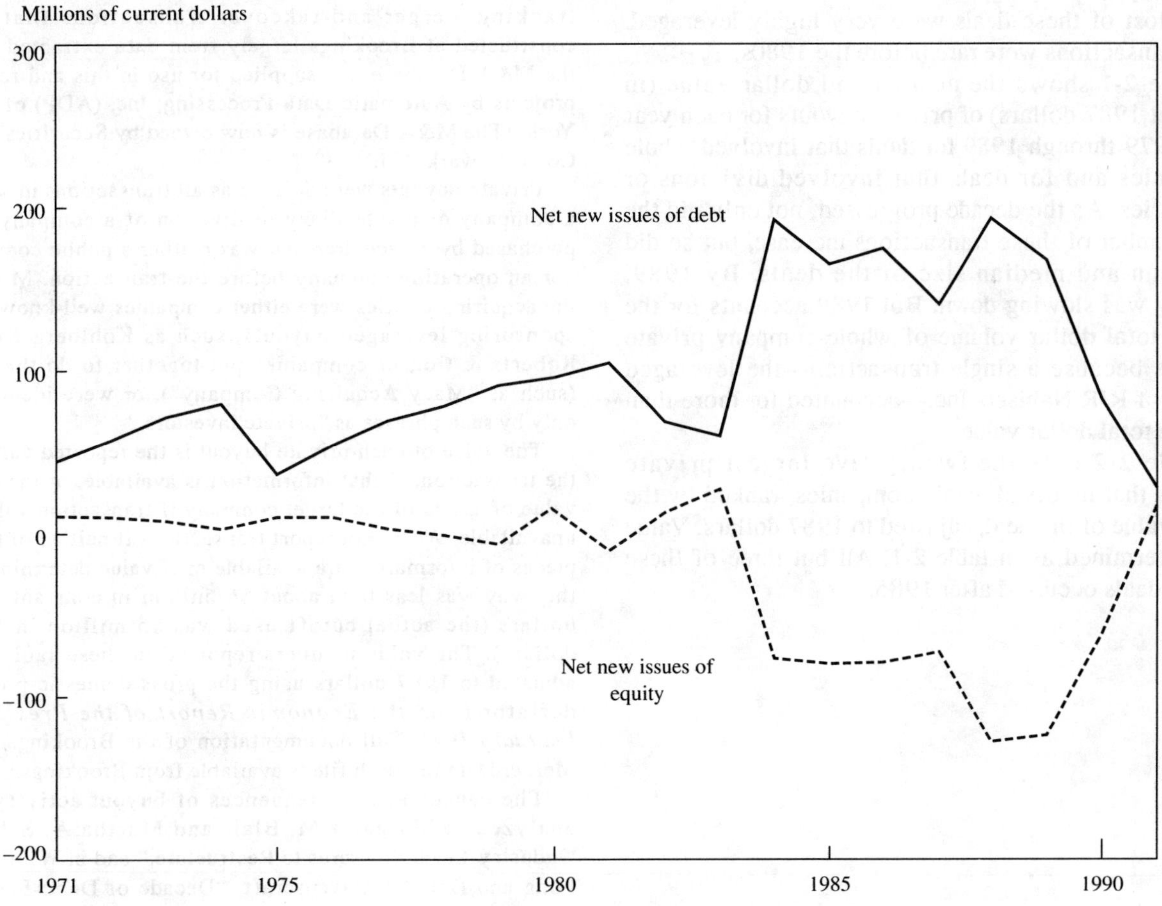

Private Buyouts

One important way equity was retired was through private buyouts, in which publicly traded companies or subsidiaries of publicly traded companies were taken private by small groups of investors or buyout sponsors. Most of these deals were very highly leveraged. Such transactions were rare before the 1980s.

Table 2-1 shows the number and dollar value (in constant 1987 dollars) of private buyouts for each year from 1979 through 1989 for deals that involved whole companies and for deals that involved divisions or subsidaries. As the decade progressed, not only did the total number of these transactions increase, but so did the mean and median size of the deals. By 1989, activity was slowing down. But 1989 accounts for the largest total dollar volume of whole-company private buyouts because a single transaction—the leveraged buyout of RJR Nabisco, Inc.—accounted for more than half the total dollar value.

Table 2-2 lists the twenty-five largest private buyouts that involved whole companies, ranked by the dollar value of the deal, adjusted to 1987 dollars. Value was determined as in table 2-1. All but three of these largest deals occurred after 1985.

Source Notes, Tables 2-1 and 2-2

Data on private buyouts are from the Brookings/ADP Merger Data research file. This is a comprehensive data set tracking merger and takeover transactions that was constructed at Brookings largely from data extracted from the M&A Database and supplied for use in this and related projects by Automatic Data Processing, Inc. (ADP) of New York. (The M&A Database is now owned by Securities Data Co. of Newark, N.J.)

Private buyouts were defined as all transactions in which a company or a subsidiary or division of a company was purchased by an acquirer that was neither a public company nor an operating company before the transaction. Most of the acquiring entities were either companies well-known for sponsoring leveraged buyouts, such as Kohlberg Kravis Roberts & Co., or companies put together to do the deal (such as "Macy Acquiring Company"), or were identified only by such phrases as "private investors."

The value of each private buyout is the reported value of the transaction, if that information is available, or the book value of assets of the target company if transaction value is unavailable. We do not report transactions if neither of these pieces of information are available or if value determined in this way was less than about $6 million in constant 1987 dollars (the actual cutoff used was $5 million in 1982 dollars). The value numbers reported in these tables are adjusted to 1987 dollars using the gross domestic product deflator from the *Economic Report of the President, February 1992*. Full documentation of the Brookings/ADP Merger Data research file is available from Brookings.

The causes and consequences of buyout activity are analyzed in Margaret M. Blair and Martha A. Schary, "Industry-Level Pressures to Restructure," and in William F. Long and David J. Ravenscraft, "Decade of Debt: Lessons from LBOs in the 1980s," both in *The Deal Decade*.

Table 2-1. Private Buyouts, U.S.-Based Companies, 1979-89
Millions of 1987 dollars

Year	Whole Companies: Number	Whole Companies: Total Value	Whole Companies: Mean	Whole Companies: Median	Divestitures: Number	Divestitures: Total Value	Divestitures: Mean	Divestitures: Median
1979	1	76.34	76.34	76.34	0	0	0	0
1980	2	220.50	110.25	110.25	2	38.63	19.32	19.32
1981	22	3921.18	178.24	43.09	30	2176.17	72.54	33.65
1982	29	4495.96	155.03	32.58	30	980.23	32.67	17.36
1983	32	3756.88	117.40	41.86	47	2869.44	61.05	35.55
1984	68	16336.10	240.24	62.09	52	4324.22	83.16	22.53
1985	73	13952.02	191.12	44.68	71	9429.27	132.81	36.02
1986	59	27763.26	470.56	113.40	108	23804.16	220.41	72.34
1987	43	26820.12	623.72	173.57	101	14397.03	142.54	50.00
1988	87	29071.57	334.16	141.03	68	15183.14	223.28	91.43
1989	63	43713.06	693.86	67.96	50	6889.39	137.79	70.11

Table 2-2. Twenty-Five Largest Whole-Company Private Buyouts, 1979-89
Millions of 1987 dollars

Rank	Year	Target	Acquiring Principals	Value
1	1989	RJR Nabisco Inc.	Kohlberg Kravis Roberts & Co.	22802
2	1986	Beatrice Cos. Inc.	Kohlberg Kravis Roberts & Co.	6450
3	1986	Safeway Stores Inc.	Kohlberg Kravis Roberts & Co.	4371
4	1987	Southland Corp.	Thompson Co.	4004
5	1987	Borg-Warner Corp.	AV Holdings Corp.	3764
6	1987	Owens-Illinois Inc.	Kohlberg Kravis Roberts & Co.	3688
7	1986	R. H. Macy & Co. Inc.	Macy Acquiring Corp.	3613
8	1988	Fort Howard Corp.	FH Acquisition Corp.	3455
9	1989	NWA Inc.	Wings Holdings Inc.	3407
10	1989	Hospital Corp. of America	TF Investments Inc.	3400
11	1984	Continental Group Inc.	Kiewit-Murdock Investment Corp.	3022
12	1988	American Standard Inc.	Kelso & Co.	2418
13	1988	Jim Walter Corp.	Hillsborough Holdings Corp. (KKR)	2345
14	1987	Burlington Industries Inc.	Burlington Holdings Inc.	2156
15	1985	Storer Communications Inc.	SCI Holdings Inc. (KKR)	1877
16	1987	Supermarkets General Corp.	SMG Acquisition Corp.	1813
17	1987	Avis Inc.	Private investors (including Avis employees)	1750
18	1987	Lear Siegler Inc.	L Acquisition Corp.	1689
19	1986	National Gypsum Co.	Anchor Holdings Inc.	1652
20	1988	Koppers Co. Inc.	BNS Inc.	1599
21	1985	Levi Strauss & Co.	HHF Corp.	1577
22	1986	Revco D. S. Inc.	Anac Holding Corp.	1534
23	1989	Jefferson Smurfit Corp.	SIBV/MS Holdings Inc.	1527
24	1989	TW Services Inc.	SWT Associates LP (Coniston Partners)	1402
25	1989	West Point-Pepperell Inc.	Farley Inc.	1401

Industry Distribution of Buyout Activity

Although private buyouts occurred in most industries or sectors of the economy, some industries were targeted more heavily than others. Table 2-3 shows private buyout activity in manufacturing and nonmanufacturing sectors. Manufacturing accounted for more than half of all private buyout activity in the 1980s (if measured by value), even though the sector accounts for only about 20 percent of economic activity.

At the level of more narrowly defined industries, the question of which were most heavily targeted depends on the measure of activity used. Table 2-4 shows the ten industries experiencing the heaviest buyout activity. Industries are ranked by the total number of buyouts involving firms in that industry, by the total dollar value (in constant 1987 dollars) of buyouts, and by the ratio of the dollar value of buyouts to a measure of the average assets in that industry during the 1980s. By any measure, radio and television broadcasting firms were leading targets for buyout activity. Fifty-seven buyouts, valued at $15.5 billion (in 1987 dollars), involved broadcasting firms. The total value of the buyouts represented almost 57 percent of the average value of assets in that industry during the 1980s.

Source Notes, Tables 2-3 and 2-4

The Brookings/ADP Merger Data research file (see source notes for tables 2-1 and 2-3) includes a four-digit standard industrial classification (SIC) code identifying the primary industry of most acquisition and buyout targets. These codes were used to assign each transaction either to manufacturing or nonmanufacturing. Industry codes were missing for eight private buyouts included in the totals in table 2-1.

Transaction counts and values were summed by year to produce totals in table 2-3. Transactions were assigned to one of ninety-six industries and summed over 1979–89 to produce the totals for the second and third columns in table 2-4. The fourth column reports the ratio of the total value from the third column to a measure of the average value of assets in each industry during the 1980s. The average value was constructed from the annual value of assets by industry reported in Internal Revenue Service, *Corporation Income Tax Returns*, Statistics of Income, pub. 79 (various years). These data were collected by Martha Schary and Sarah Lane for use in a related project. See Margaret M. Blair, Sarah J. Lane, and Martha A. Schary, "Patterns of Corporate Restructuring, 1955–1987," Brookings Discussion Papers in Economics, 91-1, January 1991. The values were converted to constant 1987 dollars and averaged over the period 1979–87 (the last year for which data were available) for each industry to produce an average value of assets for the period by industry.

Table 2-3. **Private Buyouts, Manufacturing and Nonmanufacturing Sectors, 1979-89**
Millions of 1987 dollars.

	Manufacturing				Nonmanufacturing			
Year	Number	Total Value	Mean	Median	Number	Total Value	Mean	Median
1979	0	0	0	0	1	76.34	76.34	76.34
1980	2	38.63	19.32	19.32	2	220.50	110.25	19.32
1981	34	3331.70	97.99	37.14	17	2575.54	151.50	37.14
1982	34	3367.21	99.04	29.77	23	2063.10	89.70	29.77
1983	41	2501.38	61.01	36.70	37	4106.25	110.98	36.70
1984	65	11917.23	183.34	47.14	53	8501.18	160.40	47.14
1985	58	9049.33	156.02	45.92	84	14256.48	169.72	45.92
1986	76	23210.47	305.40	96.32	91	28356.95	311.61	96.32
1987	64	19510.87	304.86	63.61	80	21706.29	271.33	63.61
1988	70	23884.00	341.20	114.29	85	20370.71	239.66	114.29
1989	57	34286.46	601.52	63.65	56	16315.98	291.36	63.65
Total	501	131097.28	...	...	509	118549.32	...	...

Table 2-4. Industries Most Heavily Targeted for Private Buyouts, 1980-89
Millions of 1987 dollars

Industry	Number of Private Buyouts	Value	Value of Buyouts/ Avg. Value of Assets
Ranked by Number			
Radio & Television Broadcasting	57	15469	0.5663
Banking	38	3892	0.0014
Miscellaneous Wholesale Trade	35	2543	0.0077
Food Prods. except Grain Mill Prods.	32	10563	0.1143
Legal, Health, Education, & Social Svcs.	31	10360	0.1393
Miscellaneous Retail Stores	30	6766	0.1021
Insurance	30	4797	0.0050
Eating & Drinking Places	26	4640	0.1054
Business Services	25	3259	0.0355
Rubber & Miscellaneous Plastic Prods.	25	2775	0.0807
Ranked by Value			
Tobacco Manufacturers	2	22939	0.4806
Radio & Television Broadcasting	57	15469	0.5663
Food Stores	24	15275	0.3236
Food Prods. except Grain Mill Prods.	32	10563	0.1143
Legal, Health, Education, & Social Svcs.	31	10360	0.1393
Paper & Allied Prods.	13	8507	0.1419
Lighting & Other Electrical Equip.	17	7691	0.0889
General Merchandise Stores	17	7614	0.0590
Automotive and Misc. Repair Svcs.	8	7057	0.2668
Misc. Retail Stores	30	6766	0.1021
Ranked by Ratio of Buyout Value to Value of Assets			
Radio & Television Broadcasting	57	15469	0.5663
Weaving Mills and Textile Finishing	12	4848	0.4883
Tobacco Manufacturers	2	22939	0.4806
Food Stores	24	15275	0.3236
Refrigeration Machinery	8	4851	0.3042
Glass, Glassware & Other Glass Prods.	9	5999	0.2814
Automotive & Misc. Repair Services	8	7057	0.2668
Womens & Childrens Clothing	9	2675	0.2596
Mens & Boys Clothing	10	2565	0.2543
Metal Cans & Shipping Containers	2	3127	0.2394

Junk Bond Issuers

Among the most controversial transactions of the deal decade were companies' issues of new, publicly traded debt securities that were below investment grade. These securities were promptly dubbed junk bonds by the media. Before the 1980s, publicly traded junk bonds were mostly bonds that had been investment grade when issued, but that were downgraded by the bond-rating services ("fallen angels") because the issuer was experiencing financial distress. These bonds did not have a large following, and pension funds, mutual funds, and other financial institutions typically avoided them.

In the 1980s, however, investment banking firms, led by Drexel Burnham Lambert, created an active market in junk bonds. Early in the decade original-issue junk bonds were primarily used as a substitute for bank debt for firms that were relatively unknown, in high-risk or start-up industries, or that for various other reasons did not have good access to public markets for investment financing. Later in the decade, firms that previously had strong credit ratings began issuing these low-rated but high-yielding bonds to finance acquisitions, buyouts, and leveraged recapitalizations.

Table 2-5 shows the number of underwritten, original-issue junk bonds issued each year during the 1980s by nonfinancial, nonelectric utility companies. The second column shows the number of different issuers involved each year, the third column the total face value of issues each year (in constant 1987 dollars), and the fourth and fifth columns the mean and median face value of junk bonds issued in each year. The annual number of issues in the last four years of the decade was five to six times the annual number in the first three years of the decade, and the annual dollar volume was more than sixteen times as great.

Table 2-6 lists the twenty-five companies most active in issuing junk bonds, ranked by the total face value (in constant 1987 dollars) issued from 1980 to 1989. More than half these issuers were financing private buyouts; the remainder were financing acquisitions or attempted acquisitions, or recapitalizing themselves as a defense against a hostile takeover attempt.

Source Notes, Tables 2-5 and 2-6

A comprehensive list of underwritten junk bonds issued by nonfinancial, nonutility companies from 1980 to 1988 was supplied to Brookings by Barrie A. Wigmore of Goldman Sachs, and a similar list of junk bonds issued in 1989 was supplied by Martin Fridson of Merrill Lynch. Both Wigmore and Fridson had compiled their lists from transactions reported by IDD Information Services, Inc. Excluded are debt issued in exchange offers and privately placed issues, previously issued junk bonds, and bonds downgraded to junk status. Wigmore describes and analyzes the 1980–88 data in "The Decline in the Credit Quality of New Issue Junk Bonds," *Financial Analysts Journal*, vol. 46 (September–October 1990), pp. 53–62. See also Peter Tufano, "Financing Acquisitions in the Late 1980s: Sources and Forms of Capital,"for a discussion of the use of specially tailored junk bonds and other instruments to finance acquisitions in the late 1980s, and Blair and Schary, "Industry-Level Pressures to Restructure," for a discussion of the causes and consequences of debt-based restructuring activity. Both are in *The Deal Decade*.

Table 2-5. Original-Issue Junk Bonds, 1980-89
Millions of 1987 dollars face value

Year	Number of Issues	Number of Issuers	Value	Mean	Median
1980	26	26	1217	47	42
1981	20	18	1507	75	68
1982	19	19	1754	92	72
1983	46	39	4139	90	74
1984	68	54	7259	107	82
1985	94	73	8538	91	64
1986	151	123	24168	160	103
1987	136	96	25241	186	125
1988	134	103	25815	193	154
1989	117	91	24451	209	139

Table 2-6. Twenty-Five Most Active Junk Bond Issuers, 1980-89
Millions of 1987 dollars face value

Rank	Issuer	Number of Issues	Face Value
1	RJR Holdings Corp. [a]	5	5637.45
2	BCI Holdings Corp. [a]	4	2579.98
3	Southland Corp. [a]	4	2199.20
4	Turner Broadcasting System Inc. [b]	8	2171.95
5	Metromedia Inc. [a, c]	9	2109.89
6	Fort Howard Corp. [a]	4	1648.70
7	Harcourt Brace Jovanovich Inc. [d]	5	1642.49
8	Wickes Cos. Inc. (New) [b]	3	1569.96
9	E-II Holdings Inc. [b, e]	2	1500.00
10	Owens-Illinois Inc. [a]	4	1443.00
11	Holiday Corp. [d]	2	1400.00
12	Burlington Holdings Inc. [a]	4	1295.00
13	Kroger Co. [d]	2	1153.14
14	American Standard Inc. [a]	2	1054.76
15	Federated Department Stores Inc. [f]	2	1042.25
16	Safeway Stores Holdings Corp. [a]	2	1031.99
17	Duracell Holdings Corp. [a]	2	1029.84
18	Charter Medical Corp. [a]	9	1022.62
19	Borg Warner Holdings Corp. [a]	2	1000.00
20	McCaw Cellular Communications Inc. [b]	2	984.99
21	CJI Industries Inc. [g]	4	931.72
22	Allied Stores Corp. [f]	2	900.00
23	Viacom Inc. [d]	3	880.73
24	TW Food Services Inc. [a]	2	841.33
25	Container Corp. of America [a, h]	3	784.13

a. Funds used to finance a private buyout.
b. Funds used to make or attempt a large acquisition.
c. Liquidated in 1986.
d. Funds used to finance a recapitalization of issuing firm, sometimes in defense against hostile takeover.
e. Subsequently acquired by American Brands Inc. in "pac-man" defense against hostile takeover.
f. Acquired by Campeau Corp. in highly-leveraged transactions.
g. Partially acquired by Triangle Industries in 1988; CJI in turn acquired all of Triangle Industries, then changed name to Triangle Industries; Triangle Industries bought by Pechiney S.A. in 1989.
h. Sold by Mobil Corp. to Jefferson Smurfit Corp.

Industry Distribution of Junk Bond Issues

Table 2-7 classifies the total number and face value (in constant 1987 dollars) of junk bond issues in each year by sector. Table 2-8 reports the industries most active in issuing junk bonds in the 1980s. Industries are ranked by the number of bond issues, the dollar volume of the issues, and the ratio of the dollar volume to a measure of average assets. The radio and television broadcasting industry is again prominent in all three lists.

Source Notes, Tables 2-7 and 2-8

Firms issuing junk bonds were assigned to industries based on four-digit SIC codes collected from the CUSIP (Committee on Uniform Security Identification Procedures) directory for each issuing firm on the Wigmore and Fridson lists (see source notes for tables 2-5 and 2-6). Average assets in each industry were computed from IRS Statistics of Income data as for table 2-4.

Table 2-7. Junk Bond Issues, Manufacturing and Nonmanufacturing Sectors, 1980-89
Millions of 1987 dollars

	Manufacturing				Nonmanufacturing			
Year	Number	Total Value	Mean	Median	Number	Total Value	Mean	Median
1980	5	174.34	34.87	41.84	17	843.10	49.59	41.84
1981	5	359.95	71.99	76.05	13	1089.99	83.85	76.05
1982	5	329.36	65.87	59.67	11	1168.26	106.21	59.67
1983	15	1232.80	82.19	74.54	20	1958.72	97.94	74.54
1984	9	813.19	90.35	109.89	36	3196.70	88.80	109.89
1985	33	3366.53	102.02	79.45	40	2789.19	69.73	79.45
1986	50	7404.02	148.08	103.20	64	8072.96	126.14	103.20
1987	46	9512.50	206.79	150.00	57	10401.00	182.47	150.00
1988	39	7985.08	204.75	192.49	44	8198.17	186.32	192.49
1989	60	14785.98	246.43	156.37	56	9605.17	171.52	156.37
Total	267	45963.75	...	...	358	47323.26	...	...

Table 2-8. Industries Most Active in Junk Bond Issues, 1980-89
Millions of 1987 dollars

Industry	Number of Issues	Value	Value of Junk Bonds/ Avg. Value of Assets
Ranked by Number			
Radio & Television Broadcasting	46	7037	0.2576
Motion Pictures, Amusement & Recreation	33	3860	0.0887
Crude Petroleum, Natural Gas Extraction	28	2934	0.0291
Real Estate	28	2396	0.0121
Food Stores	27	5781	0.1225
Air Transportation	26	2786	0.0537
Health, Legal, Education, & Social Services	26	2370	0.0319
Miscellaneous Retail Stores	25	2505	0.0378
Industrial Chemicals	16	3019	0.0259
Motor Vehicles & Equipment	16	2002	0.0145
Ranked by Value			
Radio & Television Broadcasting	46	7037	0.2576
Food Stores	27	5781	0.1225
Tobacco Manufacturers	5	5637	0.1181
Motion Pictures, Amusement & Recreation	33	3860	0.0887
General Merchandise Stores	15	3249	0.0252
Industrial Chemicals	16	3019	0.0259
Crude Petroleum, Natural Gas Extraction	28	2934	0.0291
Aircraft, Guided Missiles, & Parts	12	2834	0.0418
Air Transportation	26	2786	0.0537
Paper & Allied Products	12	2769	0.0462
Ranked by Ratio of Buyout Value to Value of Assets			
Radio & Television Broadcasting	46	7037	0.2576
Knitting Mills	5	800	0.2475
Weaving Mills & Textile Finishings	15	2352	0.2369
Leather & Leather Products	3	1609	0.2056
Books, Greeting Cards, & Misc. Publishing	9	2353	0.1555
Refrigeration Machinery	9	2332	0.1462
Food Stores	27	5781	0.1225
Tobacco Manufacturers	5	5637	0.1181
Ordnance & Accessories	2	87	0.1050
Motion Pictures, Amusement & Recreation	33	3860	0.0887

Part 3. Changing Climate for Corporate Governance

Corporate Ownership

The pattern of ownership of corporations and the legal and institutional environment that determine who has what influence in the governance of firms has never been completely settled. But the changes in these areas in the 1980s were dramatic.

Figure 3-1 and table 3-1 show how the pattern of corporate ownership has changed since World War II. Figure 3-1 shows how the total value of all corporate equities (in constant 1987 dollars) was allocated among households, financial institutions, and foreign shareholders at ten-year intervals since 1950. Total equity holdings by households were lower in real terms in 1990 than in 1970, despite a substantial increase in the total value of all equities. The difference is accounted for by the rapid growth in holdings by foreigners and institutional investors. As of 1990, financial institutions accounted for at least 36.2 percent of corporate equity holdings and foreigners accounted for another 6.5 percent.

Table 3-1 classifies equity holdings in more detail. The value of holdings (in current dollars) is reported for each year since 1946 for households, foreign shareholders, and for each of eight categories of financial institution. In the 1980s, holdings by mutual funds and state and local government pension funds grew the most relative to holdings by other financial institutions. These two categories now account for more than 40 percent of corporate equities held by financial institutions, up from 22 percent in 1980. Meanwhile, the share held by life insurers has fallen from 11.7 percent to 6.1 of all financial institution holdings, and the share held by private pension funds has fallen from 56.4 percent to 43.7 percent.

Source Notes, Figure 3-1 and Table 3-1

The Federal Reserve Board provides the longest and most consistent series of data on the distribution of holdings of corporate equities in the United States. Federal Reserve data understate the importance of financial institution holdings, however, because equities held by private trusts and endowments are counted in the household sector rather than the institutional sector.

The Institutional Investor Project of the Columbia Center for Law and Economic Studies, which has compiled its own numbers for selected years in the 1980s, estimates that equity holdings by all financial institutions, including private trusts and endowments, amounted to 38.5 percent of all equities in 1981 (versus 25.8 percent reported above), and 42.7 percent in 1986 (versus 30.6 percent reported above). See Carolyn Kay Brancato, "The Pivotal Role of Institutional Investors in Capital Markets: A Summary of Economic Research at the Columbia Institutional Investor Project," Columbia University School of Law, June 14, 1990.

The data used for figure 3-1 and table 3-1 were taken from Board of Governors of the Federal Reserve System, "Flow of Funds Accounts, Financial Assets and Liabilities Outstanding," pub. Z.1, various issues. To produce Figure 3-1, the nominal values reported in table 3-1 were adjusted to constant 1987 dollars using the gross domestic product deflator.

Figure 3-1. Ownership of Corporate Equities, 1950–90

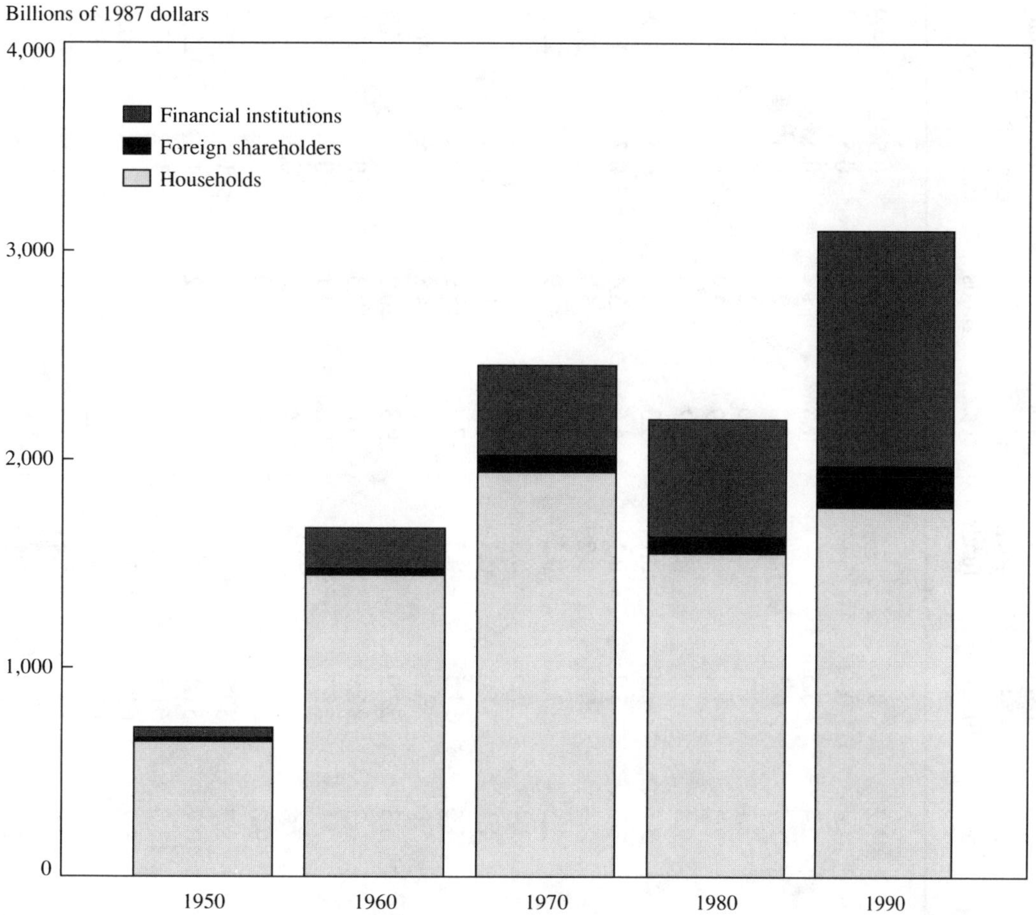

Table 3-1. Value of Corporate Equity Holdings, by Group and Institution, 1946-91
Millions of nominal dollars

Year	Households	Foreign	Comm. banks	Mutual savings banks	Life ins.	Private pension funds	State & local govt. funds	Other ins. cos.	Mutual funds	Brokers/ dealers ins.	Total fin. groups	Total
1946	102.1	2.7	--	0.2	1.2	0.3	--	1.7	1.0	0.5	4.9	109.7
1947	99.8	2.5	--	0.1	1.4	0.4	--	1.7	1.2	0.5	5.3	107.6
1948	98.6	2.3	--	0.2	1.4	0.5	--	1.8	1.2	0.5	5.6	106.5
1949	106.4	2.5	--	0.2	1.7	0.6	--	2.2	2.7	0.6	8.0	116.9
1950	130.3	2.9	--	0.2	2.1	1.1	--	2.6	2.9	0.5	9.5	142.7
1951	152.8	3.5	--	0.2	2.2	1.4	--	2.9	2.9	0.6	10.2	166.5
1952	166.5	3.7	--	0.3	2.4	1.8	0.1	3.2	3.3	0.6	11.9	182.1
1953	158.3	3.7	--	0.4	2.6	2.4	0.1	3.3	3.5	0.6	12.9	174.9
1954	228.9	5.3	--	0.6	3.3	3.2	0.1	4.5	5.4	0.7	18.7	251.9
1955	278.5	6.6	--	1.0	3.6	6.1	0.2	5.4	6.9	0.9	24.1	309.2
1956	296.0	7.0	--	1.0	3.5	7.1	0.2	5.6	7.9	0.7	25.9	328.9
1957	258.7	6.1	--	1.0	3.4	7.5	0.3	5.2	7.4	0.8	25.5	290.3
1958	360.1	8.3	--	1.4	4.1	11.6	0.4	6.7	11.7	0.5	36.3	404.7
1959	386.2	9.4	--	1.4	4.6	14.5	0.5	7.2	13.9	0.6	42.6	438.2
1960	378.4	9.3	--	1.3	5.0	16.5	0.6	7.5	14.8	0.5	46.3	434.0
1961	477.9	11.8	--	1.6	6.3	22.9	0.9	9.3	20.3	0.2	61.4	551.1
1962	416.2	10.3	--	1.5	6.3	21.9	1.0	8.6	18.3	0.3	57.9	484.4
1963	488.7	12.5	--	1.8	7.1	27.7	1.5	10.0	22.1	0.5	70.6	571.8
1964	535.7	13.8	--	2.0	7.8	33.7	2.0	11.4	25.6	0.9	83.5	633.0
1965	600.5	14.6	--	2.3	9.0	40.8	2.5	12.0	30.9	1.2	98.6	713.7
1966	540.9	12.6	--	2.0	8.7	39.5	2.8	11.0	28.9	1.3	94.3	647.8
1967	676.3	25.5	0.1	2.5	10.7	51.1	3.9	13.0	39.2	1.7	122.1	823.9
1968	806.9	29.5	0.1	2.4	13.0	61.5	5.8	14.6	46.1	1.5	145.0	981.4
1969	699.1	26.8	0.1	2.5	13.2	61.4	7.3	13.3	40.9	1.9	140.5	866.4
1970	682.7	27.2	0.1	2.8	14.6	67.1	10.1	13.2	39.7	2.0	149.5	859.4
1971	778.0	30.8	0.1	3.5	20.0	88.7	15.4	16.6	48.6	2.1	194.9	1003.7
1972	862.0	39.1	0.1	4.5	26.5	107.8	22.2	21.8	51.7	2.4	237.0	1138.1
1973	663.6	33.5	0.2	4.2	25.4	93.6	20.2	19.7	38.3	2.8	204.3	901.4
1974	459.9	24.2	0.2	3.7	21.3	74.8	16.4	12.8	26.3	2.2	157.6	641.7

1975	598.6	35.3	0.2	4.4	27.5	108.0	24.3	14.2	33.7	3.4	215.6	849.5
1976	712.9	42.9	0.2	4.4	33.7	125.5	30.1	16.9	37.3	1.5	249.7	1005.5
1977	668.5	39.8	0.2	4.8	32.3	123.6	30.0	17.1	31.9	1.8	241.7	950.0
1978	663.9	42.1	0.1	4.8	35.1	150.3	33.3	19.4	31.7	1.9	276.5	982.5
1979	812.2	48.3	0.1	4.7	38.9	175.4	37.1	24.8	35.4	2.6	319.0	1179.5
1980	1111.3	64.6	0.1	4.2	46.3	223.5	44.3	32.3	42.4	3.3	396.4	1572.3
1981	1051.2	64.4	0.1	3.2	46.2	218.5	47.8	32.4	37.4	3.5	389.1	1504.7
1982	1184.0	76.3	0.1	3.3	52.9	251.2	60.2	38.5	49.4	4.9	460.4	1720.7
1983	1334.5	96.4	0.1	4.3	62.2	302.0	89.6	48.1	74.4	10.0	590.7	2021.6
1984	1343.6	96.1	--	4.1	60.3	286.4	96.5	44.7	80.6	8.9	581.5	2021.2
1985	1700.0	125.6	0.1	5.2	74.0	374.0	120.1	57.0	113.7	14.1	758.1	2583.7
1986	1877.1	168.9	0.1	7.0	76.4	427.3	150.2	61.2	161.2	17.7	901.1	2947.1
1987	1750.9	175.6	--	7.0	80.5	423.8	169.6	65.1	181.7	10.7	938.4	2864.9
1988	1876.6	201.0	--	8.5	89.3	475.2	219.7	71.4	187.6	12.2	1064.0	3141.6
1989	2205.1	260.6	4.7	11.0	106.5	583.8	300.1	94.3	239.5	14.1	1354.0	3819.7
1990	2007.8	228.3	2.2	8.8	106.6	537.1	296.1	85.4	224.3	9.6	1270.1	3506.2
1991	2238.4	290.5	4.5	10.3	111.0	798.7	386.6	104.6	399.2	14.3	1829.1	4358.0

Takeover Laws

Battles for control of public corporations were fought out not only in boardrooms and on stock exchange floors in the 1980s, but also in the courtrooms and state legislatures. Table 3-2 identifies fifteen important court rulings and laws (or groups of laws) that altered the way takeover battles were fought and continue to influence how public corporations are governed.

Source Notes, Table 3-2

Table 3-2 was prepared by Mark Roe, Columbia University Law School. It summarizes information in Roe, "Takeover Politics," in *The Deal Decade*.

Table 3-2. Key Rulings and Changes in Takeover Laws, 1968-90

1968 **Williams Act**	Congress prohibits "fraudulent, deceptive or manipulative acts or practices in connection with any tender offer."
Pre-1982 **First Generation State Anti-Takeover Statutes**	States require offerors to file with the state, require bidders to wait before commencing offers, sometimes allow the state administrator to determine the fairness of offers and stop them if they are unfair.
December 23, 1981 **Mobil Corp. v. Marathon Oil**	A federal circuit court holds that a "crown jewel" defense used by Marathon Oil is a prohibited manipulative act under the Williams Act.
June 23, 1982 **Edgar v. MITE**	The Supreme Court holds first-generation takeover statutes unconstitutional.
June 1983 **Lenox's Poison Pill**	Takeover target issues preferred stock that would dilute (or "poison") a takeover. Thereafter poison pills become widespread.
June 4, 1985 **Schreiber v. Northern Burlington**	The Supreme Court, unlike lower court in Marathon in 1981, declares that the term "manipulative" only includes lying or rigged bidding and not most takeover tactics. Federal courts would no longer play a key role in determining the validity of takeover tactics.
November 19, 1985 **Moran v. Household Int'l**	The Delaware court validates the issuance of a "poison pill," a powerful antitakeover defense.
March 13, 1986 **Revlon, Inc. v. MacAndrews & Forbes**	A Delaware court requires the auction of a company once some kind of sale becomes inevitable.

July 17, 1986 **"All Holders" Rule**	The SEC preempts a state law allowing a secondary takeover defense.
Mid-1980s **2d Generation** **State Antitakeover** **Statutes**	These control-share statutes require that when a shareholder obtains a big proportion of shares, the other shareholders get to vote on whether the new controling shareholder could vote.
April 21, 1987 **CTS Corp. v.** **Dynamics Corp.**	The Supreme court holds that the Williams Act does not preempt control-share, second-generation state antitakeover laws.
1987 Wave of **Antitakeover** **Statutes**	After CTS, many states pass laws protecting companies within their borders.
Late 1980s **3d Generation** **State Antitakeover** **Statutes**	State legislatures expand the corporate constituencies the directors can, or must, consider beyond shareholders.
February 26, 1990 **Paramount Comm.** **v. Time Inc.**	A Delaware court allows Time's board to reject an offer from Paramount without presenting it to the shareholders. Instead, the board merges with Warner at a lower price but with managerial continuity.
1990 **Delaware** **Antitakeover** **Statute**	Delaware passes a moratorium rule prohibiting many offerors from merging with the target for three years after buying a stake.

Corporate Constituency Laws

There continues to be as much controversy over what caused the takeover movement to subside at the end of the 1980s as there was over what caused it to boil up in the first place. But a crucial factor, some scholars have argued, was a round of state laws enacted late in the 1980s that specifically authorized managers and directors to consider the impact of takeovers on corporate constituents other than shareholders. Table 3-3 lists the twenty-nine states that have passed these "other stakeholder" or "corporate constituency" laws, and outlines what the laws require. Although a few states had corporate constituency language in their corporation laws before 1987, most of these laws were passed later.

Corporate constituency laws generally give management broad leeway to reject takeover proposals. Delaware, where about half of all publicly traded corporations are chartered, has not so far enacted a specific corporate constituency law. But many legal scholars interpret the ruling of the Delaware Supreme Court in *Paramount Communications* v. *Time Inc.* in 1990 as giving management of Delaware-chartered firms leeway similar to that of corporations chartered in other states.

Source Notes, Table 3-3

Updated and reprinted from the appendix to Steven M. H. Wallman, "The Proper Interpretation of Corporate Constituency Statutes and Formulation of Director Duties," *Stetson Law Review*, vol. 21 (Fall 1991), pp. 163–96. Effective dates of statutes were added at Brookings under Wallman's supervision.

Table 3-3. States with Corporate Constituency Laws, as of 1992

State	Code and Section Number	Effective Date	Board may consider nonshareholder constituencies (shareholders must be considered)	Board may consider nonshareholder constituencies (shareholders not listed)	Shareholders as one of several groups that board may consider	Board shall consider various factors	Other
Arizona	Ariz. Rev. Stat. Ann. § 10-1202	7-22-87					X[1]
Connecticut	Conn. Gen. Stat. §33-313(e)	6-7-88				X[2, 3]	
Florida	Fla. Stat. § 607.111(9); §607.0830(3)	6-22-89 6-27-89			X		
Georgia	Ga. Code Ann. § 14-2-202(b)(5)	7-1-89	X[4]				
Hawaii	Haw. Rev. Stat. § 415-35(b)	6-7-89	X				
Idaho	Idaho Code § 30-1702	3-22-88	X				
Illinois	Ill. Rev. Stat. ch. 32, para. 8.85	8-23-85		X			
Indiana	Ind. Code § 23-1-35-1(d), (f) &(g)	4-1-86			X[5]		
Iowa	Iowa Code §491.101B	12-31-89	X[2]				
Kentucky	Ky. Rev. Stat. Ann. § 271B.12-210(4)	7-15-88	X				

Table 3-3 (continued)

State	Code and Section Number	Effective Date	Board may consider nonshareholder constituencies (shareholders must be considered)	Board may consider nonshareholder constituencies (shareholders not listed)	Shareholders as one of several groups that board may consider	Board shall consider various factors	Other
Louisiana	La. Rev. Stat. Ann. § 12:92(G)(2)	7-10-88	X[2]				
Maine	Me. Rev. Stat. Ann. tit. 13-A, § 716	9-19-85	X				
Massachusetts	Mass. Gen. L. Ch. 156B, § 65	7-18-89			X[6]		
Minnesota	Minn. Stat. § 302A.251(5)	6-1-87			X[6]		
Mississippi	Miss. Code Ann. § 79-4-8.30(d)	7-1-90	X				
Missouri	Mo. Rev. Stat. § 351.347.1(4)	5-6-86			X[2,7]		
Nebraska	Neb. Rev. Stat. § 21-2035(1)(c)	4-9-88		X			
New Jersey	N.J. Stat. Ann. § 14A:6-1(2); § 14A:6-14(4)	6-29-89 2-4-89	X				
New Mexico	N.M. Stat. Ann. § 53-11-35(D)	4-9-87	X				
New York	N.Y. Bus. Corp. Law § 717(b)	6-30-89			X		
Nevada	Nevada Gen. Corp. Law § 78.138(3)	10-1-91			X		
Ohio	Ohio Rev. Code Ann. § 1701.13(F)(7); § 1701.59(D)	11-22-86 10-10-84	X				
Oregon	Or. Rev. Stat. § 60.357(5)	3-5-89			X[2, 6]		

Pennsylvania	15 Pa. Cons. Stat. § 1715; § 1716	12-19-90 12-23-83		X (§1716)	X[5](§1715)		
Rhode Island	R.I. Gen. Laws § 7-5.2-8	7-3-90	X[2]				
South Dakota	S.D. Codified Laws Ann. § 47-33-4	7-1-90	X[2]				
Tennessee	Tenn. Code. Ann. § 48-35-204	3-11-88		X[2, 4, 8]			
Wisconsin	Wis. Stat. § 180.0827	6-13-87	X				
Wyoming	Wyo. Stat. §§ 17-16-830; 17-18-201 to 17-18-203	1-1-90 3-11-89	X (§ 17-16-830)				X[9] (§ 17-18-201 to 203)

1. Shall consider the long-term and short-term interests of the corporation and its shareholders--no other groups listed.
2. Takeover context only.
3. Shall consider the long-term and short-term interests of shareholders and other groups.
4. Charter opt-in.
5. Statute explains that no groups' interest need be considered dominant.
6. Shareholders at end of list.
7. Not shareholders per se, but current and future value of corporation.
8. Registered corporations only.
9. Bondholder protection only.

Shareholder Participation

Even as the states were passing laws that seemed to tilt the balance of power in corporate governance in favor of management, individual and institutional shareholders were making more attempts to influence management. Table 3-4 presents the numbers of shareholder proposals submitted and voted on at annual meetings of U.S. corporations each year since 1978.

Shareholder proposals first became important in the late 1970s and early 1980s when religious groups and other social activists began using their voting power as investors to try to influence corporate policies on environmental issues, investments in third world countries, gender and racial bias, and health and safety matters. Corporate gadflies (individual shareholders with small holdings) also began to use their franchise to try to affect corporate governance. In 1979–80, for example, five individual proponents or coordinated groups of small shareholders were responsible for 409 of the 873 shareholder proposals submitted. Religious groups were responsible for another 96. Such proposals rarely got much of a hearing and even more rarely garnered a significant share of the votes. Proposals requiring firms to disinvest from South Africa were a notable exception.

In the early 1980s the Securities and Exchange Commission tightened the rules governing submission of proposals by shareholders, and the number fell from a high of 983 in the 1980–81 proxy season to 442 during the 1984–85 season. By the mid-1980s, however, corporate governance issues again become important as hostile takeover activity increased. The number of proposals submitted climbed to 973 in the 1990–91 proxy season, and institutional investors became more involved. They used shareholder resolutions as a way to influence the outcome of takeover battles—by encouraging firms to enact bylaws prohibiting greenmail, for example. Proposals from institutional investors have continued to be important every year since the 1986–87 proxy season, with issues such as confidential proxy voting, elimination of antitakeover measures, and withdrawal from or sanctions against South Africa dominating the agendas of these investor groups.

Table 3-4 also shows the average favorable vote for proposals that were submitted to a vote. These numbers, however, understate the influence of proposals submitted by institutional investors in recent years. First, the ability of these investors to influence a large share of the vote means that their proposals are more likely to be submitted for a vote and more likely to win a higher percentage of the vote than proposals submitted by individual shareholders. Second, some active institutional investors have begun meeting directly with management, sometimes withdrawing their proposals when conciliatory agreements are reached before the proposals come to a vote.

Source Notes, Table 3-4

Data for proxy years 1980–81 through 1991–92 came from summary tables in annual issues of "Report on Shareholder Proposals" of the American Society of Corporate Secretaries, Inc., New York. Data for earlier years were compiled at Brookings from records provided by the society. For these earlier years, average favorable votes for each category were computed as averages of the average favorable vote reported for each specific type of proposal within the category, weighted by the number of proposals of each type that were voted on. The American Society of Corporate Secretaries collects shareholder resolution information annually by surveying its members (including representatives of about 2,000 public companies in the United States and Canada) and examining Securities and Exchange Commission records. Theirs are the most consistent, comprehensive, and long-running data available on shareholder resolutions.

Table 3-4. Shareholder Resolutions, by Subject, Presented at U.S. Corporation Annual Meetings, 1978-92

	1991-92			1990-91			1989-90		
Subject	Total number of proposals	Number voted on	Average percentage vote for	Total number of proposals	Number voted on	Average percentage vote for	Total number of proposals	Number voted on	Average percentage vote for
Directors and Directors Meetings	177	96	20.70	192	121	21.10	134	80	19.70
Shareholders and Changes of Ownership	96	48	33.90	149	66	38.90	125	54	32.10
Compensation and Benefit Plans	106	44	18.20	110	39	19.40	65	19	18.00
Annual Meetings and Proxy Material	77	38	29.80	76	45	29.60	62	43	31.20
Management and Employees	28	7	9.40	39	10	12.60	29	6	7.50
Auditors and Accounting Issues	3	1	16.20	7	3	9.20	6	1	20.20
Subtotal	487	234	24.06	573	284	25.93	421	203	24.92
Energy (Other than Nuclear)	5	3	7.00	--	--	--	--	--	--
Public Responsibility Issues	61	30	5.30	83	30	5.10	67	18	5.70
Nuclear Power	4	4	10.00	9	7	7.50	9	4	8.20
Environmental Issues	99	41	8.00	98	46	7.70	46	17	7.60
Foreign Involvement	146	88	9.90	165	113	11.40	141	94	11.40
Political Issues	5	5	8.50	6	3	7.60	9	7	6.40
Corporate Contributions	3	3	8.40	1	1	3.30	6	1	4.00
Subtotal	323	174	8.60	362	200	9.37	278	141	9.82
Miscellaneous Proposals	53	6	12.90	38	3	17.40	40	3	22.00
Total	863	414		973	487	--	739	347	--

Table 3-4 (continued)

	1988-89			1987-88			1986-87		
Subject	Total number of proposals	Number voted on	Average percentage vote for	Total number of proposals	Number voted on	Average percentage vote for	Total number of proposals	Number voted on	Average percentage vote for
Directors and Directors meetings	115	83	16.70	123	79	14.90	57	43	11.70
Shareholders and Changes of Ownership	94	38	25.80	79	35	26.00	134	58	21.60
Compensation and Benefit Plans	59	4	11.00	44	7	7.10	35	9	11.00
Annual Meetings and Proxy Material	61	43	19.00	27	22	12.40	18	9	7.20
Management and Employees	40	12	5.60	42	12	5.20	34	9	7.90
Auditors and Accounting Issues	5	1	3.50	2	1	6.90	5	4	4.80
Subtotal	374	181	18.22	317	156	15.89	283	132	15.23
Energy (Other than Nuclear)	--	--	--	--	--	--	--	--	--
Public Responsibility Issues	41	27	5.70	40	28	5.50	24	11	4.90
Nuclear Power	7	7	7.20	9	7	7.30	9	4	9.00
Environmental Issues	6	4	3.60	6	2	5.10	13	6	6.30
Foreign Involvement	132	107	11.20	165	122	10.40	182	115	11.10
Political Issues	19	19	6.10	11	9	5.00	9	8	5.00
Corporate Contributions	8	7	4.10	8	8	5.20	10	8	3.50
Subtotal	213	171	9.13	239	176	8.92	247	152	9.69
Miscellaneous Proposals	26	0	--	14	0	--	20	3	10.10
Total	613	352	--	570	332	--	550	287	--

	1985-86			1984-85			1983-84		
Subject	Total number of proposals	Number voted on	Average percentage vote for	Total number of proposals	Number voted on	Average percentage vote for	Total number of proposals	Number voted on	Average percentage vote for
Directors and Directors Meetings	78	52	10.45	77	62	10.05	86	66	9.92
Shareholders and Changes of Ownership	97	35	12.59	76	27	13.81	80	38	9.91
Compensation and Benefit Plans	31	13	6.59	50	12	10.24	53	28	6.29
Annual Meetings and Proxy Material	12	6	6.40	23	11	4.16	36	19	5.32
Management and Employees	31	8	6.21	33	9	10.40	57	24	4.91
Auditors and Accounting Issues	27	3	5.50	16	1	2.28	6	4	7.00
Subtotal	276	117	10.04	275	122	5.74	318	179	8.12
Energy (Other than Nuclear)	--	--	--	--	--	--	7	--	--
Public Responsibility Issues	24	11	4.52	22	13	5.35	41	9	4.81
Nuclear Power	19	9	5.99	21	6	8.75	25	10	9.26
Environmental Issues	8	4	7.46	9	4	5.69	5	--	--
Foreign Involvement	87	61	10.90	57	25	8.40	50	30	5.62
Political Issues	15	14	4.23	23	14	5.08	31	11	4.94
Corporate Contributions	10	8	4.33	12	9	4.71	15	11	4.33
Subtotal	163	107	8.34	144	71	6.60	174	71	5.72
Miscellaneous Proposals	16	--	--	23	3	15.66	17	2	4.88
Total	455	224	--	442	196	--	509	252	--

Table 3-4 (continued)

	1982-83			1981-82			1980-81		
Subject	Total number of proposals	Number voted on	Average percentage vote for	Total number of proposals	Number voted on	Average percentage vote for	Total number of proposals	Number voted on	Average percentage vote for
Directors and Directors Meetings	145	109	8.06	190	142	9.10	200	138	7.22
Shareholders and Changes of Ownership	117	49	10.33	127	47	8.94	131	47	6.98
Compensation and Benefit Plans	97	47	5.71	97	46	7.81	95	57	6.83
Annual Meetings and Proxy Material	94	58	4.31	75	45	4.97	53	39	5.59
Management and Employees	79	47	4.87	86	46	4.27	81	55	4.79
Auditors and Accounting Issues	19	12	7.92	23	14	10.49	37	15	5.53
Subtotal	551	322	6.92	598	340	7.76	597	351	6.49
Energy (Other than Nuclear)	8	5	6.22	12	7	4.85	13	9	5.73
Public Responsibility Issues	78	22	3.7	16	9	4.90	12	10	6.95
Nuclear Power	48	30	5.28	69	42	5.28	49	38	4.51
Environmental Issues	10	4	4.17	3	3	4.03	16	6	4.37
Foreign Involvement	97	55	5.01	80	41	4.26	87	48	4.44
Political Issues	28	20	2.35	81	27	4.49	97	54	4.13
Corporate Contributions	39	18	4.64	100	35	5.69	98	38	4.29
Subtotal	308	154	4.50	361	164	4.92	372	203	4.52
Miscellaneous Proposals	11	2	2.58	14	4	3.67	14	5	3.80
Total	870	478	--	973	508	--	983	559	--

	1979-80			1978-79			1977-78		
Subject	Total number of proposals	Number voted on	Average percentage vote for	Total number of proposals	Number voted on	Average percentage vote for	Total number of proposals	Number voted on	Average percentage vote for
Directors and Directors meetings	174	129	9.70	156	109	8.69	173	122	9.88
Shareholders and Changes of Ownership	103	49	8.17	97	41	7.49	94	51	8.47
Compensation and Benefit Plans	91	60	7.31	90	65	10.41	105	76	8.16
Annual Meetings and Proxy Material	81	59	8.52	116	67	11.62	74	38	14.36
Management and Employees	55	38	7.11	71	45	5.83	73	56	4.85
Auditors and Accounting Issues	40	21	15.22	11	6	7.58	12	9	20.00
Subtotal	544	356	8.9	541	333	9.06	531	352	9.24
Energy (Other than Nuclear)	16	7	6.47	5	3	7.63	1	1	2.20
Public Responsibility Issues	36	21	1.96	58	12	5.33	64	28	3.92
Nuclear Power	37	26	6.02	10	4	6.45	6	3	6.20
Environmental Issues	14	6	5.92	3	1	4.50	--	--	--
Foreign Involvement	63	39	3.54	74	44	3.45	66	36	6.59
Political Issues	17	13	4.66	9	8	6.04	22	18	5.91
Corporate Contributions	132	73	4.19	41	26	6.10	12	9	5.09
Subtotal	315	185	4.23	200	98	4.8	171	95	5.47
Miscellaneous Proposals	14	4	3.78	38	8	11.72	30	13	19.04
Total	873	545	--	779	439	--	705	457	--

4. Mergers and Acquisitions in the Postwar Era

Acquisitions of U.S.-Based Companies

Economic historians have identified four great waves of corporate mergers and takeovers since the emergence of large corporations in the United States in the late nineteenth century. The first occurred in the 1890s, when numerous small and mid-sized industrial firms consolidated to form giant industrial monopolies such as Standard Oil, U.S. Steel, U.S. Rubber, International Harvester, and Pittsburgh Plate Glass. The second occurred in the 1920s as smaller firms consolidated to form large firms (such as Bethlehem Steel) that could compete in the same industries with some of the monopoly firms formed in the previous wave.

Brookings has compiled comprehensive data on merger and takeover activity covering the last two great merger waves. Table 4-1 lists the total number and value of all 1955–89 acquisitions of U.S.-based companies with a known value of $6 million or more (in constant 1987 dollars). Private buyouts, reported in section 2, are excluded. Acquisitions are valued at either the value of the transaction, if that is known, or the book value of the target firm's assets if transaction value is unknown, and all values are adjusted to constant 1987 dollars using the GDP deflator. The merger wave of the late 1960s and the wave of the 1980s are evident in this series. The real dollar volume of acquisitions reached a peak in 1968 that was not surpassed until 1981. The merger wave of the 1980s peaked in 1986.

Source Notes, Table 4-1

This table and those that follow were generated by splicing together the Brookings Historical Merger Data file, covering 1955–79, and the Brookings/ADP Merger Data research file, covering 1979–89. The former was constructed by compiling and reconciling data from three primary sources, including two computerized data files from the Federal Trade Commission and a large collection of handwritten files given to Brookings by the University of Texas College of Business Administration for use in this project. Records were also checked against standard references and directories such as Compustat, *Moody's Industrial Manual* (New York: Moody's Investors' Service, various years), and the CUSIP Directory to add, confirm, and correct information. The resulting file contains records of 4,252 acquisitions and divestitures. Full documentation of this data file, as well as copies of the file, can be obtained from Brookings.

The Brookings/ADP file, described briefly in the source notes for tables 2-1 and 2-2, contains records of 7,899 acquisitions, divestitures, and private buyouts from 1979 through 1989. This file was extracted from raw data files of the M&A Database, which were made available to Brookings for use in this project by Automatic Data Processing, Inc. (ADP) of New York. The M&A Database is now owned by Securities Data Co. of Newark, N.J. These data were cleaned to eliminate very small transactions and transactions that did not result in a change of control of the target company. Information was added at Brookings to categorize transactions by type. Full documentation of this file is available from Brookings. Securities Data has agreed to entertain proposals by other scholars to use this cleaned research file by special arrangement with Securities Data and Brookings.

Summary statistics from preliminary versions of both merger data files were reported in Blair, Lane, and Schary, "Patterns of Corporate Restructuring, 1955–1987." Both files have been substantially revised since then.

Table 4-1. Acquisitions of U.S.-Based Companies, 1955-89
Millions of 1987 dollars

Year	Number	Value	Mean	Median
1955	114	16895.20	148.20	65.50
1956	94	9945.15	105.80	52.74
1957	75	5408.16	72.11	53.06
1958	82	5628.00	68.63	40.00
1959	132	9574.22	72.53	39.06
1960	102	7553.85	74.06	50.00
1961	113	14114.07	124.90	45.63
1962	100	10627.99	106.28	55.97
1963	121	13125.37	108.47	41.18
1964	154	12084.84	78.47	36.10
1965	166	14580.11	87.83	35.21
1966	230	17803.06	77.40	27.21
1967	352	35564.36	101.04	33.00
1968	438	54391.49	124.18	31.55
1969	427	42030.77	98.43	21.02
1970	230	24602.63	106.97	28.49
1971	178	11834.10	66.48	29.73
1972	199	12001.06	60.31	25.77
1973	168	11659.00	69.40	24.21
1974	124	11717.06	94.49	32.65
1975	99	7056.67	71.28	34.55
1976	120	11368.05	94.73	34.42
1977	162	15983.79	98.67	35.78
1978	201	24945.40	124.11	46.43
1979	442	51388.96	116.26	30.92
1980	349	41784.62	119.73	34.54
1981	533	78508.60	147.30	26.62
1982	516	71194.81	137.97	30.07
1983	529	64754.27	122.41	31.83
1984	645	109806.53	170.24	29.63
1985	745	113327.53	152.12	37.08
1986	1097	162863.10	148.46	41.28
1987	805	111668.47	138.72	38.23
1988	614	145517.55	237.00	54.67
1989	429	107887.48	251.49	57.17

Industry Distribution of Acquisition Targets

Table 4-2 classifies acquisitions into those in which the target firm was a manufacturing company and those in which the target was a nonmanufacturing company. Acquisitions of nonmanufacturing targets accounted for more than two-thirds of all acquisitions (59 percent by dollar volume) in the 1980s. In earlier years, manufacturing firms represented a larger share of the targets.

Are some industries more acquisition-prone than others? Comparisons of how acquisition activity is distributed across industries leads to different conclusions depending on the time period selected and the measure of activity used. Table 4-3 shows the industries in which acquisitions were most frequent before 1979 and from 1979 to 1989, ranking the industries by the number of acquisitions, the total value of acquisitions, and the ratio of the total value of acquisitions to a measure of the average value of assets in the industry during the time period.

Before 1979 the engines and turbines industry was the only one to make all three top ten lists. In the 1980s the financial industries—banking, insurance, and holding companies and investment trusts—accounted for large numbers of targets and high dollar volume. When activity is ranked by the size of the industries' assets, however, financial industries are no longer among the most active. By any measure, radio and television broadcasting and crude petroleum and natural gas extraction firms were highly sought after as acquisitions in the 1980s. And relative to their size, manufacturing industries were nearly as heavily targeted in the 1980s as they had been in the previous twenty-five years, with six manufacturing industries making the top ten list for 1979–89 as opposed to eight among the top ten in 1955–78.

Source Notes, Tables 4-2 and 4-3

Both of the merger data sets used to construct the tables in this section (see the source notes for table 4-1) include four-digit SIC codes identifying the primary industry of target companies, acquiring companies, and, in the case of divestitures, the divesting parent companies. For table 4-2, transactions were assigned to manufacturing or nonmanufacturing based on the industry code for targets. Codes are missing for about 6 percent of target firms in data for 1955–79 but fewer than 0.2 percent of target firms in the data for the 1980s. Source data sets and selection criteria for data from 1955 to 1979 may have underrepresented transactions involving nonmanufacturing firms, but the extent of this bias is unknown.

For table 4-3 the four-digit SIC codes for targets were used to assign each transaction to one of ninety-six industries. Transaction counts and values were then summed by industry over all years within each subperiod to produce the counts and values. The measure of average assets by target industry was constructed from data on book value of assets, by industry, reported in annual editions of IRS Statistics of Income, as explained in the source notes for tables 2-4 and 2-8. Asset values for each year were converted to constant 1987 dollars using the GDP deflator and then averaged for 1955–78 and separately for 1979–87 (1987 was the last year for which data were available). These averages were then used in the denominators of the ratios reported in columns four and eight.

These ratios mean, for example, that for 1979–89 the total value of all acquisitions of firms in the radio and television broadcasting industry exceeded the average value of assets in that industry in the same period. This does not necessarily imply that every radio and television broadcaster was acquired during the period. Instead, the assets that were acquired may have sold at more than their book value, and some properties may have changed hands more than once.

Table 4-2. Acquisition Targets, Manufacturing and Nonmanufacturing Sectors, 1955-89
Millions of 1987 dollars

	Manufacturing				Nonmanufacturing			
Year	Number	Value	Mean	Median	Number	Value	Mean	Median
1955	100	15895.20	158.95	65.50	8	554.59	69.32	65.50
1956	79	8303.80	105.11	54.85	8	1358.65	169.83	54.85
1957	68	4722.45	69.45	53.06	6	657.14	109.52	53.06
1958	64	4580.00	71.56	48.00	12	816.00	68.00	48.00
1959	105	7175.78	68.34	42.97	20	1789.06	89.45	42.97
1960	82	5450.00	66.46	50.00	12	1807.69	150.64	50.00
1961	86	10406.84	121.01	45.63	22	3463.88	157.45	45.63
1962	73	7314.93	100.20	59.70	23	3122.76	135.77	59.70
1963	89	9368.01	105.26	40.44	26	3437.50	132.21	40.44
1964	124	7888.09	63.61	36.10	24	3918.77	163.28	36.10
1965	130	13370.60	102.85	35.21	33	1153.17	34.94	35.21
1966	188	12500.34	66.49	27.21	33	5190.48	157.29	27.21
1967	288	28788.78	99.96	33.00	49	5508.25	112.41	33.00
1968	345	42814.71	124.10	37.85	71	10838.61	152.66	37.85
1969	308	38349.97	124.51	27.03	79	2719.83	34.43	27.03
1970	174	19011.18	109.26	28.49	46	5221.08	113.50	28.49
1971	124	8284.18	66.81	35.14	43	3071.54	71.43	35.14
1972	126	7410.86	58.82	25.77	51	3213.92	63.02	25.77
1973	117	7527.93	64.34	24.21	37	3835.67	103.67	24.21
1974	84	6431.07	76.56	31.18	25	4584.43	183.38	31.18
1975	72	4776.18	66.34	34.55	17	1754.07	103.18	34.55
1976	92	8025.80	87.24	34.42	22	2242.83	101.95	34.42
1977	124	11744.07	94.71	33.99	30	3720.93	124.03	33.99
1978	137	18693.68	136.45	49.75	48	5679.58	118.32	49.75

Table 4-2 (continued)

	Manufacturing				Nonmanufacturing			
Year	Number	Value	Mean	Median	Number	Value	Mean	Median
1979	222	25587.12	115.26	37.56	202	25398.79	125.74	37.56
1980	130	13714.90	105.50	36.26	216	28000.27	129.63	36.26
1981	178	18875.21	106.04	28.20	351	59467.04	169.42	28.20
1982	148	24623.51	166.38	34.37	367	46548.63	126.84	34.37
1983	159	16705.75	105.07	24.66	369	48031.89	130.17	24.66
1984	173	29513.31	170.60	25.98	468	80244.67	171.46	25.98
1985	214	56979.79	266.26	39.45	528	56279.33	106.59	39.45
1986	407	71882.63	176.62	40.25	684	90785.26	132.73	40.25
1987	264	45902.46	173.87	50.00	537	65172.21	121.36	50.00
1988	212	60580.97	285.76	64.24	400	84850.02	212.13	64.24
1989	181	67041.41	370.39	63.65	247	40822.09	165.27	63.65

Table 4-3. Industries Most Heavily Targeted for Acquisitions, 1955-78, 1979-89
Value in millions 1987 dollars

1955-78				1979-89			
Industry	Number	Value	Value Of Acquisitions/ Avg. Value Of Assets	Industry	Number	Value	Value Of Acquisitions/ Avg. Value Of Assets
Ranked by number							
Food Prods. except Grain Mill Prods.	228	19282	0.6079	Banking	1206	134289	0.0482
Paper & Allied Prods.	156	18783	0.8709	Holding Companies & Investment Trusts	552	66860	0.1298
Miscellaneous Wholesale Trade	138	7566	0.0915	Business Services	287	24791	0.2703
Lighting & Other Electrical Equip.	130	8885	0.4098	Radio & Television Broadcasting	249	30252	1.1075
Industrial Chemicals	124	13631	0.4382	Insurance	240	36039	0.0372
Misc. Manufacturing	110	4800	0.5161	Health, Legal, Educational Services	225	19266	0.2591
Engines & Turbines	104	14036	1.9935	Crude Petroleum, Natural Gas	172	77999	0.7724
Farm & Construction Machinery	95	7883	0.4673	Miscellaneous Wholesale Trade	158	14467	0.0439
Primary Nonferrous Metal	94	8298	0.3200	Office Computing & Accounting Mach.	125	13889	0.1538
Rubber & Misc. Plastic Prods.	94	3803	0.2975	Food Prods. except Grain Mill Prods.	122	46725	0.5055
Ranked by value							
Petroleum & Coal Prods.	63	27087	0.2379	Banking	1206	134289	0.0482
Food Prods. except Grain Mill Prods.	228	19282	0.6079	Crude Petroleum, Natural Gas	172	77999	0.7724
Paper & Allied Prods.	156	18783	0.8709	Holding Companies & Investment Trusts	552	66860	0.1298
Crude Petroleum, Natural Gas	92	18244	1.1695	Drugs	76	46886	0.9113
Primary Iron & Steel	78	18127	0.5835	Food Prods. except Grain Mill Prods.	122	46725	0.5055
Engines & Turbines	104	14036	1.9935	Insurance	240	36039	0.0372
Industrial Chemicals	124	13631	0.4382	Radio & Television Broadcasting	249	30252	1.1075
Motor Vehicles & Equip.	81	12663	0.2177	Business Services	287	24791	0.2703
Radio, Television & Commun. Equip.	90	9992	0.7441	Securities, Real Estate & Insurance	122	24028	0.0954
Office Computing & Accounting Machines	54	9399	0.4254	Electric, Gas & Sanitary Service	83	23694	0.0464
Ranked by ratio of value of acquisitions to value of assets							
Engines & Turbines	104	14036	1.9935	Radio & Television Broadcasting	249	30252	1.1075
Optical, Medical & Ophthalmic Goods	59	5681	1.8053	Drugs	76	46886	0.9113
Coal Mining	39	7056	1.3389	Iron Ore Mining	2	2763	0.8625
Scientific Instruments	61	6406	1.2520	Nonferrous Metal Mining	25	10733	0.8059
Crude Petroleum, Natural Gas	92	18244	1.1695	Scientific Instruments	118	12191	0.7780
Mens & Boys Clothing	64	5298	1.1317	Crude Petroleum, Natural Gas	172	77999	0.7724
Agricultural & Other Chemical Prods.	77	8680	1.0921	Books, Greeting Cards & Misc. Pub.	37	11178	0.7388
Metalworking Machinery	67	4870	1.0106	Optical, Medical & Ophthalmic Goods	102	11809	0.7232
Refrigeration Machinery	77	5660	0.9927	Household Appliances	26	7670	0.6619
Cuttlery, Hand Tools and Hardware	55	3993	0.9258	Ordnance & Accessories	6	498	0.5985

Industry Distribution of Acquirers

Table 4-4 classifies acquisitions by whether the acquiring firm was in the manufacturing or nonmanufacturing sector. Acquirers in the nonmanufacturing sector accounted for nearly two-thirds of all acquisition activity (53 percent by dollar volume) in the 1980s. Manufacturing firms were more prominent as acquirers in earlier years.

Table 4-5 lists the top ten acquiring industries in each subperiod, ranked as in table 4-3. Before 1979, manufacturing industries in general were prominent as acquirers. Radio, television, and communications equipment and aircraft, guided missiles, and parts were the only industries to make all three top ten lists. In 1979–89, firms in the financial industries (holding companies and investment trusts, banks, and insurance companies) accounted for a large share of acquisitions, by either count or value. But when acquisition activity is measured by the size of the acquiring industry, no financial industries remain in the top ten. The crude petroleum and natural gas extraction industry and the radio and television broadcasting industry were major acquirers by all three measures.

Source Notes, Tables 4-4 and 4-5.

For table 4-4 see source notes for table 4-2. Transactions are assigned to sectors based on the industry code of the acquiring firm. Industry codes of acquiring firms are missing for 4.5 percent of the acquisitions listed in the 1955–78 data and 0.5 percent of acquisitions in the 1979–89 data.

Like table 4-3, table 4-5 ranks industries by the ratio of the dollar volume of acquisition activity to a measure of average assets of the acquirer industry constructed from industry data in the IRS *Statistics of Income*. See also Source Notes for tables 2-3 and 2-4. For small industries a few acquisitions can have a very significant effect on this ratio. By this measure, for example, firms in the ordnance and accessories industry made acquisitions totaling more than 1.6 times the average value of assets in that industry during the 1980s.

Table 4-4. Acquisitions, Manufacturing and Nonmanufacturing Sector Acquirers, 1955-89
Millions of 1987 dollars

Year	Manufacturing				Nonmanufacturing			
	Number	Value	Mean	Median	Number	Value	Mean	Median
1955	93	15358.08	165.14	65.5	12	1174.67	97.89	65.50
1956	82	9194.09	112.12	54.85	5	485.23	97.05	54.85
1957	62	4383.67	70.70	53.06	4	628.57	157.14	53.06
1958	74	5016.00	67.78	40.00	6	592.00	98.67	40.00
1959	85	7843.75	92.28	58.59	9	757.81	84.20	58.59
1960	89	6173.08	69.36	50.00	6	469.23	78.21	50.00
1961	100	12311.79	123.12	45.63	5	330.80	66.16	45.63
1962	81	8328.36	102.82	55.97	14	1874.25	133.88	55.97
1963	98	11283.46	115.14	44.12	11	694.85	63.17	44.12
1964	133	10413.36	78.30	32.49	15	1577.62	105.17	32.49
1965	129	12113.56	93.90	35.21	29	2244.72	77.40	35.21
1966	198	15239.12	76.97	23.81	23	2193.88	95.39	23.81
1967	311	30739.27	98.84	29.70	33	2458.75	74.51	29.70
1968	376	41839.44	111.28	28.39	55	11362.78	206.60	28.39
1969	358	28384.29	79.29	21.02	54	13072.91	242.09	21.02
1970	186	18804.63	101.10	24.22	40	5663.82	141.60	24.22
1971	135	9045.38	67.00	32.43	39	2081.68	53.38	32.43
1972	166	10096.42	60.82	25.77	31	1860.82	60.03	25.77
1973	122	8138.42	66.71	20.40	37	2728.81	73.75	20.40
1974	99	8002.47	80.83	25.41	22	3484.00	158.36	25.41
1975	78	6050.57	77.57	34.55	19	941.06	49.53	34.55
1976	98	9771.50	99.71	33.93	20	1506.69	75.33	33.93
1977	123	9857.64	80.14	32.20	33	5595.89	169.57	32.20
1978	152	18213.41	119.83	47.26	42	6278.48	149.49	47.26
1979	245	27601.22	112.66	33.59	193	23728.20	122.94	33.59
1980	146	15850.05	108.56	34.87	202	25924.81	128.34	34.87
1981	197	32540.04	165.18	27.88	333	45478.07	136.57	27.88
1982	157	27476.61	175.01	40.57	357	43686.54	122.37	40.57
1983	180	19329.30	107.38	27.01	347	45286.26	130.51	27.01
1984	211	52442.97	248.54	30.22	432	57318.51	132.68	30.22
1985	246	56346.74	229.05	39.01	498	56967.71	114.39	39.01
1986	413	77738.61	188.23	40.76	678	82886.21	122.25	40.76
1987	269	47003.61	174.73	52.13	529	63984.97	120.95	52.13
1988	221	73433.15	332.28	64.13	391	70375.69	179.99	64.13
1989	164	63624.39	387.95	62.73	261	43729.06	167.54	62.73

Table 4-5. Industries Most Active as Acquirers, 1955-78, 1979-89
Value in millions 1987 dollars

1955-78				1979-89			
Industry	Number	Value	Value of Acquisitions/ Avg. Value of Assets	Industry	Number	Value	Value of Acquisitions/ Avg. Value of Assets
Ranked by number							
Food Prods. except Grain Mill Prods.	345	21847	0.6888	Holding Companies & Investment Trusts	1534	137531	0.2669
Petroleum & Coal Prods.	184	37406	0.3285	Banking	339	58872	0.0211
Industrial Chemicals	182	19394	0.6235	Insurance	227	25822	0.0267
Radio, Television, & Comm. Equip.	180	19279	1.4357	Business Services	201	18749	0.2044
Paper & Allied Prods.	162	13453	0.6237	Radio & Television Broadcasting	196	24115	0.8828
Lighting & Other Electrical Equip.	161	10557	0.4869	Crude Petroleum, Natural Gas	195	63401	0.6278
Holding Companies & Investment Trusts	157	18035	0.2228	Health, Legal, Educational Services	194	13008	0.1749
Motor Vehicles & Equipment	136	11917	0.2049	Food Prods. except Grain Mill Prods.	134	29612	0.3204
Lumber & Wood Prods.	111	9363	0.6158	Newspapers & Periodicals	127	20476	0.4978
Aircraft, Guided Missiles, & Parts	104	18699	0.9165	Electric, Gas, & Sanitary Service	127	26422	0.0517
Ranked by value							
Petroleum & Coal Prods.	184	37406	0.3285	Holding Companies & Investment Trusts	1534	137531	0.2669
Food Prods. except Grain Mill Prods.	345	21847	0.6888	Crude Petroleum, Natural Gas	195	63401	0.6278
Industrial Chemicals	182	19394	0.6235	Banking	339	58872	0.0211
Radio, Television, & Comm. Equip.	180	19279	1.4357	Petroleum & Coal Prods.	40	36223	0.0757
Aircraft, Guided Missiles, & Parts	104	18699	0.9165	Motor Vehicles & Equipment	91	36044	0.2612
Holding Companies & Investment Trusts	157	18035	0.2228	Drugs	109	30441	0.5917
Crude Petroleum, Natural Gas	55	16446	1.0543	Food Prods. except Grain Mill Prods.	134	29612	0.3204
Paper & Allied Prods.	162	13453	0.6237	Industrial Chemicals	101	28133	0.2416
Drugs	95	12964	1.0745	Beverages	61	27235	0.5101
Motor Vehicles & Equipment	136	11917	0.2049	Electric, Gas, & Sanitary Services	127	26422	0.0517
Ranked by ratio of value of acquisitions to value of assets							
Household Appliances	63	7587	1.5151	Ordnance & Accessories	8	1335	1.6048
Radio, Television, & Comm. Equip	180	19279	1.4357	Iron Ore Mining	10	4983	1.5555
Engines & Turbines	102	9926	1.4097	Household Appliances	41	16812	1.4509
Soaps, Detergents, & Toilet Goods	47	6635	1.1503	Radio & Television Broadcasting	196	24115	0.8828
Drugs	95	12964	1.0745	Photographic Equipment & Supplies	24	8188	0.6866
Crude Petroleum, Natural Gas	55	16446	1.0543	Crude Petroleum, Natural Gas	195	63401	0.6278
Tobacco Manufacturers	43	9056	0.9731	Soaps, Detergents, & Toilet Goods	43	19464	0.6211
Weaving Mills & Textile Finishings	90	7035	0.9309	Drugs	109	30441	0.5917
Aircraft, Guided Missiles, & Parts	104	18699	0.9165	Hotels & Other Lodging Places	34	15500	0.5231
Metal Cans & Shipping Containers	42	3475	0.9161	Beverages	61	27235	0.5101

Whole-Company Targets and Divestitures

Table 4-6 classifies all acquisitions of U.S.-based companies into those in which the target was a whole company and those in which it was a subsidiary or division being divested from a parent company. Divestitures large enough to satisfy the size cutoff for this analysis (about $6 million in constant 1987 dollars) were unusual before the 1980s, but by the second half of the decade they represented one-third of all transactions (29 percent by dollar volume).

Some scholars have argued that a driving force of the 1980s takeover wave was the effort to dismantle conglomerate firms put together in the previous takeover wave and redeploy their assets to more valuable uses. Table 4-6 confirms that divestiture activity was very important in the 1980s. Two other tables provide evidence on this explanation of the 1980s merger wave. Table 4-10 categorizes all acquisitions of U.S. companies by whether they were horizontal, vertical, or unrelated, and table 4-14 lists the companies that were most actively divesting units during the 1980s.

Table 4-7 further classifies acquisitions into whole-company targets that were publicly traded and those that were not. In the peak three years of the 1960s merger wave (1967–69), acquisitions of public companies accounted for 26 percent of all transactions (55 percent by dollar volume). At the time that was exceptional because most acquisitions had previously targeted nonpublic companies. Since then, acquisitions of public companies have continued to dominate activity, accounting for just over half of all whole-company acquisitions (79 percent by dollar volume) in the 1980s.

Source Notes, Tables 4-6 and 4-7

All target firms in both data sets used to construct these tables were coded for whether they were whole companies or units of larger companies being divested. Whole companies were further identified as public or nonpublic. Since 1970 any company was considered public if it had a CUSIP (Committee on Uniform Security Identification Procedures) number. CUSIP codes were developed in the mid-1960s by the New York Clearing House Association to provide a unique identification code for all publicly traded securities. For data older than 1970 we relied on coding in the source data sets to identify publicly traded targets. See the source notes for table 4-1 for more detail. Full documentation of the data sets used to construct these tables is available from Brookings.

Table 4-6. Whole-Company Targets and Divestitures, 1955-89
Millions of 1987 dollars

	Whole companies				Divestitures			
Year	Number	Value	Mean	Median	Number	Value	Mean	Median
1955	109	16655.02	152.80	65.50	5	240.17	48.03	30.57
1956	91	9763.71	107.29	50.63	3	181.43	60.48	59.07
1957	73	5363.27	73.47	53.06	2	44.90	22.45	22.45
1958	78	5408.00	69.33	42.00	4	220.00	55.0	36.00
1959	129	9519.53	73.79	39.06	3	54.69	18.23	7.81
1960	99	7488.46	75.64	50.00	3	65.38	21.79	19.23
1961	112	14102.66	125.92	45.63	1	11.41	11.41	11.41
1962	97	10430.22	107.53	55.97	3	197.76	65.92	82.09
1963	113	12470.96	110.36	44.12	8	654.41	81.80	33.09
1964	149	11767.15	78.97	36.10	5	317.69	63.54	28.88
1965	161	14323.07	88.96	35.21	5	257.04	51.41	35.21
1966	222	17534.35	78.98	27.21	8	268.71	33.59	22.11
1967	345	33303.63	96.53	29.70	7	2260.73	322.96	95.71
1968	422	53195.91	126.06	31.55	16	1195.58	74.72	72.56
1969	405	39481.22	97.48	21.02	22	2549.55	115.89	40.54
1970	202	18124.20	89.72	25.64	28	6478.43	231.37	48.43
1971	162	10407.07	64.24	27.03	16	1427.03	89.19	47.30
1972	182	10611.89	58.31	25.77	17	1389.18	81.72	56.70
1973	145	9879.34	68.13	21.79	23	1779.66	77.38	48.43
1974	108	9557.37	88.49	31.53	16	2159.69	134.98	44.54
1975	84	6009.92	71.55	33.54	15	1046.75	69.78	40.65
1976	110	10092.72	91.75	37.28	10	1275.33	127.53	23.90
1977	145	14846.04	102.39	35.78	17	1137.75	66.93	23.26
1978	185	23565.64	127.38	48.09	16	1379.77	86.24	31.51
1979	419	48083.96	114.76	29.92	23	3305.00	143.70	53.44
1980	319	35437.13	111.09	32.08	30	6347.49	211.58	36.61
1981	413	68346.74	165.49	26.49	120	10161.86	84.68	28.83
1982	396	62967.12	159.01	31.86	120	8227.69	68.56	25.95
1983	386	53972.36	139.82	31.51	143	10781.91	75.40	32.11
1984	485	89617.88	184.78	28.57	160	20188.65	126.18	32.69
1985	531	85533.46	161.08	33.14	214	27794.07	129.88	44.39
1986	724	112677.52	155.63	37.69	373	50185.58	134.55	46.44
1987	496	69289.50	139.70	34.60	309	42378.96	137.15	45.00
1988	398	105472.80	265.01	54.67	216	40044.75	185.39	54.43
1989	291	84322.80	289.77	55.98	138	23564.68	170.76	60.65

Table 4-7. Public and Nonpublic Whole-Company Targets, 1955-89
Millions of 1987 dollars.

Year	Public companies				Nonpublic companies			
	Number	Value	Mean	Median	Number	Value	Mean	Median
1955	10	1807.86	180.79	113.54	99	14847.16	149.97	65.50
1956	9	1303.80	144.87	92.83	82	8459.92	103.17	46.41
1957	5	632.65	126.53	93.88	68	4730.61	69.57	51.02
1958	7	784.00	112.00	68.00	71	4624.00	65.13	40.00
1959	7	1339.84	191.41	42.97	122	8179.69	67.05	39.06
1960	8	811.54	101.44	88.46	91	6676.92	73.37	50.00
1961	9	1254.75	139.42	41.83	103	12847.91	124.74	45.63
1962	17	2157.84	126.93	81.72	80	8272.39	103.40	54.10
1963	15	1995.22	133.01	69.85	98	10475.74	106.90	38.60
1964	28	3658.84	130.67	64.08	121	8108.30	67.01	28.88
1965	19	2136.45	112.44	63.38	142	12186.62	85.82	31.69
1966	27	4043.54	149.76	23.81	195	13490.82	69.18	27.21
1967	58	10382.84	179.01	72.61	287	22920.79	79.86	26.40
1968	103	27359.95	265.63	78.86	319	25835.96	80.99	22.08
1969	148	32030.77	216.42	78.08	257	7450.45	28.99	15.02
1970	83	13953.26	168.11	45.58	119	4170.94	35.05	17.09
1971	60	7266.53	121.11	50.00	102	3140.54	30.79	18.92
1972	58	4928.90	84.98	38.66	124	5682.99	45.83	20.62
1973	68	7862.39	115.62	39.95	77	2016.95	26.19	14.53
1974	64	8399.24	131.24	50.11	44	1158.13	26.32	13.36
1975	48	4672.52	97.34	43.70	36	1337.40	37.15	14.23
1976	70	8207.44	117.25	53.54	40	1885.28	47.13	21.03
1977	100	13244.97	132.45	55.46	45	1601.07	35.58	21.47
1978	137	21918.87	159.99	71.31	48	1646.77	34.31	19.07
1979	250	41467.19	165.87	47.63	169	6616.77	39.15	14.96
1980	173	27496.73	158.94	46.72	146	7940.41	54.39	22.52
1981	172	47205.16	274.45	42.90	241	21141.58	87.72	16.48
1982	216	47605.22	220.39	55.55	180	15361.89	85.34	18.79
1983	182	37112.52	203.91	55.28	204	16859.84	82.65	19.75
1984	250	76266.05	305.06	48.35	235	13351.83	56.82	19.34
1985	262	72280.83	275.88	59.92	269	13252.64	49.27	21.30
1986	320	83126.78	259.77	64.40	404	29550.74	73.15	23.25
1987	219	52541.07	239.91	70.44	277	16748.43	60.46	20.70
1988	251	83272.47	331.76	61.80	147	22200.33	151.02	44.74
1989	183	76378.50	417.37	81.30	108	7944.30	73.56	32.43

The Largest Acquisitions

Table 4-8 lists the fifty largest acquisitions of U.S.-based companies from 1955 to 1989. Transactions are ranked by their value in constant 1987 dollars. Only five of these deals occurred before the 1980s. Twelve were acquisitions by foreign companies.

Source Notes for Table 4-8

Names of acquiring companies are for the year of the transaction.

Table 4-8. Fifty Largest Acquisitions of U.S.-Based Companies, 1955-89
Inflation adjusted value in millions of 1987 dollars

Rank	Year	Target company	Acquiring company	Inflation – adjusted value	Nominal value
1	1984	Gulf Corp.	Standard Oil Co. of California [a]	14615	13300
2	1988	Kraft Inc.	Philip Morris Cos. Inc.	12170	12644
3	1989	Squibb Corp.	Bristol-Myers Co. [b]	11556	12526
4	1984	Getty Oil Co.	Texaco Inc.	11126	10125
5	1981	Conoco Inc.	E. I. du Pont de Nemours & Co.	8776	6924
6	1989	SmithKline Beckman Corp.	Beecham Group PLC	7638	8279
7	1982	Marathon Oil Co.	U.S. Steel Corp.	7339	6150
8	1989	Marion Laboratories Inc.	Dow Chemical Co.	6531	7079
9	1986	RCA Corp.	General Electric Co.	6338	6142
10	1984	Superior Oil Co.	Mobil Corp.	6264	5700
11	1988	Federated Department Stores Inc.	Campeau Corp. [c]	6262	6506
12	1985	General Foods Corp.	Philip Morris Inc. [d]	5961	5628
13	1979	Belridge Oil Co.	Shell Oil Co.	5578	3653
14	1969	Sinclair Oil Corp.	Atlantic Richfield Co.	5559	1851
15	1989	Pillsbury Co.	Grand Metropolitan PLC	5312	5758
16	1985	Nabisco Brands Inc.	R. J. Reynolds Industries Inc. [e]	5195	4905
17	1985	Signal Cos. Inc.	Allied Corp. [f]	5139	4851
18	1988	Farmers Group Inc.	B.A.T. Industries PLC	4975	5169
19	1988	Sterling Drug Inc.	Eastman Kodak Co.	4902	5093
20	1986	Sperry Corp.	Burroughs Corp. [g]	4574	4432
21	1984	First Federal Savings & Loan Assoc.	Citicorp	4537	4129
22	1982	New York Bank for Savings	Buffalo Savings Bank [h]	4057	3400
23	1985	American Hospital Supply Corp.	Baxter Travenol Laboratories Inc. [i]	3922	3703

Table 4-8 (continued)

Rank	Year	Target company	Acquiring company	Inflation – adjusted value	Nominal value
24	1986	Allied Stores Corp.	Campeau Corp. [c]	3712	3597
25	1986	American Broadcasting Cos. Inc	Capital Cities Communications Inc. [j]	3643	3530
26	1981	Texasgulf Inc.	Societe Nationale Elf Aquitaine	3473	2740
27	1986	Kiewit Continental Inc.	Willamette Industries Inc.	3220	3120
28	1981	McMoran Oil & Gas Co.	Freeport Minerals Co. [k]	3219	2540
29	1989	Columbia Pictures Entertainment Inc.	Sony Corp.	3208	3478
30	1981	Santa Fe International Corp.	Kuwait Petroleum Corp.	3131	2470
31	1987	Viacom International Inc.	National Amusements Inc.	3107	3107
32	1987	Chesebrough-Pond's Inc.	Unilever NV	3095	3095
33	1986	Texas Oil & Gas Co.	U.S. Steel Corp [l]	3093	2997
34	1983	Bendix Corp.	Allied Corp. [f]	3088	2693
35	1969	Youngstown Sheet & Tube Co	Lykes Corp [m]	3081	1026
36	1985	Carnation Co.	Nestle SA	3065	2894
37	1984	Esmark Inc.	Beatrice Foods Co. [n]	2978	2710
38	1989	Texas Eastern Corp.	Panhandle Eastern Corp.	2972	3222
39	1989	A. H. Robins Co. Inc.	American Home Products Corp.	2939	3186
40	1985	G. D. Searle & Co.	Monsanto Co.	2878	2717
41	1984	Electronic Data Systems Corp.	General Motors Corp.	2858	2601
42	1986	MidCon Corp.	Occidental Petroleum Corp.	2772	2686
43	1982	Cities Service Co.	Occidental Petroleum Corp.	2757	2310
44	1969	Scientific Data Systems Inc	Xerox Corp	2733·	910
45	1987	Celanese Corp.	Hoechst AG [o]	2724	2724
46	1968	Sunray D X Oil Co	Sun Co Inc.	2650	840
47	1983	Southern Pacific Co.	Santa Fe Industries Inc. [p]	2638	2300
48	1985	American Natural Resources Co.	Coastal Corp.	2600	2454
49	1988	Firestone Tire & Rubber Co.	Bridgestone Corp.	2562	2562
50	1988	MacMillan Inc.	Maxwell Communication Corp. PLC	2543	2642

a) Now Chevron Corp.
b) Now Bristol-Myers Squibb Co.
c) Federated Dept. Stores and Allied States filed Chapter 11 bankruptcy, January, 1990
d) Now Philip Morris Cos. Inc.
e) Now RJR Nabisco Holdings after 1989 leveraged buyout
f) Now Allied-Signal Inc.
g) Now Unisys Corp.
h) Now Goldome Bank for Savings
i) Now Baxter International Inc.
j) Now Capital Cities/ABC Inc.
k) Now Freeport-McMoran Inc.
l) Now USX Corp.
m) Acquired by LTV Corp. in 1978
n) Taken private in leveraged buyout in 1986
o) Now Hoechts Celanese Corp.
p) Became Santa Fe Southern Pacific Corp. in 1983; now Santa Fe Pacific Corp.

Foreign Acquirers and Targets

Foreign companies became a much more important part of merger and acquisition activity in the 1980s than they had been earlier. Table 4-9 classifies acquisitions of U.S. companies since 1979 as those in which the acquirer was another U.S. company and those in which the acquirer was a foreign company. In the last half of the 1980s, acquisitions by foreigners grew to 14 percent of all acquisitions of U.S. companies (22.6 percent by dollar volume), up from 9.7 percent during 1979–84 (8.8 percent by dollar volume). For comparison, table 4-9 also shows the number and value of U.S. companies' acquisitions of foreign companies. U.S. firms acquired more and larger foreign companies in the second half of the decade than they did in the first half. But since 1985 acquisitions of foreign firms by U.S. firms have been one-fourth the number of acquisitions of U.S. firms by foreign firms (and only 16.7 percent by dollar volume).

Source Notes, Table 4-9

Transactions appear in the two files used to construct these tables only if either the acquirer or the target was a U.S.-based company. Coverage of transactions involving foreign firms was spotty and not considered reliable before 1979, so totals for those years are not reported.

Table 4-9. Foreign Acquisitions of U.S. Targets and U.S. Acquisitions of Foreign Targets, 1979-89
Millions of 1987 dollars

	U.S acquisitions of U.S. targets				Foreign acquisitions of U.S. targets				U.S. acquisitions of foreign targets			
Year	Number	Value	Mean	Median	Number	Value	Mean	Median	Number	Value	Mean	Median
1979	382	45477.34	119.05	27.41	60	5911.62	98.53	44.81	15	887.39	59.16	24.43
1980	298	36131.96	121.25	31.03	51	5652.66	110.84	41.56	11	1280.61	116.42	47.70
1981	474	66587.61	140.48	25.35	59	11920.99	202.05	42.21	11	592.40	53.85	48.16
1982	471	66803.29	141.83	27.45	45	4391.52	97.59	55.97	11	743.56	67.60	24.11
1983	507	63316.72	124.89	31.65	22	1437.55	65.34	35.61	22	1761.92	80.09	16.06
1984	591	102314.86	173.12	28.57	54	7491.68	138.73	39.56	26	1672.02	64.31	28.57
1985	687	102025.13	148.51	34.76	58	11302.40	194.87	66.21	29	1924.67	66.37	19.04
1986	967	138466.38	143.19	40.17	130	24396.71	187.67	57.26	36	2257.71	62.71	43.09
1987	698	82092.11	117.61	33.63	107	29576.36	276.41	101.00	35	6030.61	172.30	28.00
1988	498	103229.85	207.29	52.75	116	42287.71	364.55	62.14	13	4495.97	345.84	43.31
1989	320	70747.66	221.09	46.13	109	37139.82	340.73	127.71	24	9487.40	395.31	69.88

Horizontal, Vertical, and Unrelated Acquisitions

Table 4-10 shows acquisitions of U.S-based companies by whether the acquisitions were horizontal, vertical, or unrelated. One popular argument about the forces behind the last two merger waves is that the 1960s wave was driven by the creation of large conglomerates and the 1980s wave was driven by an effort to break up the conglomerates and redeploy their assets to higher-value uses.

Before the start of the 1960s merger wave in 1965, transactions in which the acquirer and target had neither a horizontal nor a vertical relationship accounted for 54 percent of all acquisitions (55 percent by dollar volume). This rose to 67 percent (66 percent by dollar volume) from 1965 to 1970. Throughout the 1970s the share of unrelated acquisitions stayed at the same level (67 percent by count and 68.5 percent by dollar volume). But in the 1980s, unrelated acquisitions accounted for only 54 percent of all acquisitions (by count and dollar volume), about the same share as in the 1950s and early 1960s. Meanwhile, horizontal transactions—in which the acquirer and target are in the same industry—accounted for 39 percent of all acquisitions (37 percent by dollar volume) in the 1980s, a higher share than in any other period covered by these data.

Source Notes, Table 4-10

Acquisitions were classified as horizontal or vertical on the basis of the primary industry codes of the acquirer and the target. If the code of the acquirer was the same as the code of the target, the transaction was considered horizontal. To define vertical relationships, input-output tables for the U.S. economy were used to determine all industry pairs for which one of the industries provided at least 10 percent of the inputs into the other industry, or for which one of the industries bought at least 10 percent of the output of the other industry. These industry pairs were developed by Martha Schary at Boston University for use in a related project. See Blair, Lane, and Schary, "Patterns of Corporate Restructuring, 1955–1987." All transactions that involved these industry pairs (but that were not horizontal) were identified as vertical. All other transactions were considered unrelated. About 4.6 percent of the transactions were missing industry codes for the acquirer or the target or both; thus their type could not be determined. No attempt was made to evaluate actual buying and selling relationships between the firms involved in each transaction, nor were possible relationships among secondary industries of these firms considered.

Table 4-10. Horizontal, Vertical, and Unrelated Acquisitions, 1955-89
Millions of 1987 dollars

Year	Horizontal				Vertical				Unrelated			
	Number	Value	Mean	Median	Number	Value	Mean	Median	Number	Value	Mean	Median
1955	52	9344.98	179.71	67.69	14	1410.48	100.75	104.80	33	5331.88	161.57	65.50
1956	30	3852.32	128.41	67.51	9	1320.68	146.74	50.63	41	4223.63	103.02	54.85
1957	27	1742.86	64.55	53.06	8	502.04	62.76	48.98	30	2738.78	91.29	55.10
1958	33	1796.00	54.42	40.00	17	1768.00	104.00	40.00	24	1812.00	75.50	54.00
1959	30	3207.03	106.90	62.50	15	683.59	45.57	35.16	43	4179.69	97.20	62.50
1960	28	1834.62	65.52	44.23	15	1557.69	103.85	88.46	44	2953.85	67.13	50.00
1961	25	2304.18	92.17	53.23	13	1159.70	89.21	57.03	62	8935.36	144.12	43.73
1962	27	2667.91	98.81	63.43	7	1470.15	210.02	93.28	57	5874.25	103.06	44.78
1963	19	2402.94	126.47	44.12	11	1110.29	100.94	44.12	74	8215.07	111.01	44.12
1964	30	1602.89	53.43	28.88	19	1909.75	100.51	61.37	94	8207.58	87.31	39.71
1965	40	5285.21	132.13	35.21	24	1697.18	70.72	26.41	91	7319.55	80.43	35.21
1966	50	3773.13	75.46	27.21	35	2190.48	62.59	27.21	127	11357.14	89.43	27.21
1967	38	2458.75	64.70	33.00	62	7825.08	126.21	33.00	231	22468.65	97.27	33.00
1968	53	5847.00	110.32	28.39	63	6476.28	102.80	37.85	294	40219.63	136.80	34.70
1969	63	5448.65	86.49	27.03	64	11506.62	179.79	15.02	247	23847.27	96.55	24.02
1970	40	6634.14	165.85	37.04	33	2865.16	86.82	28.49	143	14598.77	102.09	28.49
1971	30	2263.69	75.46	37.84	23	1989.56	86.50	32.43	111	6619.75	59.64	27.03
1972	34	2103.09	61.86	33.51	22	453.61	20.62	15.46	119	8024.26	67.43	28.35
1973	24	1713.92	71.41	32.69	17	1950.83	114.75	60.53	104	6907.09	66.41	23.00
1974	20	1265.03	63.25	31.18	9	1090.65	121.18	55.68	78	8473.77	108.64	28.95
1975	16	1180.89	73.81	39.63	15	788.38	52.56	34.55	56	4495.93	80.28	33.54
1976	27	2872.83	106.40	34.42	19	3116.63	164.03	57.36	66	4189.29	63.47	33.46
1977	29	2988.98	103.07	30.41	19	1676.21	88.22	30.41	101	10602.30	104.97	37.57
1978	28	3925.15	140.18	32.34	29	4424.40	152.57	79.60	121	15570.19	128.68	48.09
1979	108	9381.09	86.86	32.90	48	3957.52	82.45	25.34	265	37599.97	141.89	32.06
1980	109	15668.49	143.75	32.08	45	5583.65	124.08	32.08	191	20453.26	107.09	36.26
1981	170	19781.68	116.36	26.24	28	5344.98	190.89	32.32	329	52732.70	160.28	26.49
1982	187	32054.11	171.41	38.19	25	1214.80	48.59	41.17	302	37894.25	125.48	27.98
1983	192	26105.89	135.97	36.20	30	4089.13	136.30	32.68	304	34403.91	113.17	28.77
1984	242	49468.57	204.42	32.14	35	16108.01	460.23	17.80	362	44136.36	121.92	29.84
1985	299	31898.00	106.68	31.78	47	10768.92	229.13	75.00	395	70579.11	178.68	38.45
1986	446	68339.11	153.23	43.86	78	14732.52	188.88	63.41	563	77490.62	137.64	36.12
1987	353	49940.10	141.47	37.00	50	9159.97	183.20	52.77	391	51294.70	131.19	37.49
1988	235	44429.06	189.06	50.82	63	11830.51	187.79	53.83	312	87462.71	280.33	60.81
1989	186	36804.65	197.87	52.16	37	6166.93	166.67	70.09	201	64357.87	320.19	61.81

Active Acquirers

A characteristic common to the merger waves of the 1960s and 1980s is that the number of acquisitions made per active acquiring firm increases. Table 4-11 shows the number of acquisitions in each year and the number of different firms making these acquisitions. It also shows the ratio of acquisitions per acquirer and the average value of acquisitions per acquirer. These data suggest that merger waves are driven in part by a few firms that make many acquisitions. This was more true in the 1960s merger wave than in the 1980s. For example, 230 firms were responsible for the 438 acquisitions of U.S. companies in 1968, a ratio of 1.9 acquisitions per acquirer. This ratio did not reach similar peaks in the 1980s merger wave, though it rose above its typical level in the 1970s.

Table 4-12 lists the twenty-five most active acquiring companies for 1955–78, and table 4-13 lists the twenty-five most active for 1979–89. In each table, companies are ranked by the total value (in constant 1987 dollars) of acquisitions made over the period. The company names reported in table 4-12 are the names that applied as of 1978; those reported in table 4-13 are as of 1991, or the last year of the company's existence as a public company. Only three companies made both lists (Mobil Corp., Occidental Petroleum Corp, and R. J. Reynolds Industries, Inc., which became RJR Nabisco, Inc., in 1985 and was ultimately taken private in a leveraged buyout in 1989). Five of the most active acquirers in the 1979–89 period were foreign firms.

Source Notes, Tables 4-11, 4-12, and 4-13

For table 4-11 acquisitions were aggregated by name of the acquiring company in each year to determine the number of active acquiring companies, acquisitions per acquirer, and average value per acquirer.

For tables 4-12 and 4-13 acquisitions were aggregated by firm name. For the period before 1978 we made a major effort to keep track of name changes for firms so that a consistent name could be used. For 1979–89, name changes were tracked for the large acquirers but not for all firms. Moody's Investor's Service, *Moody's Industrial Manual*, various years, was the primary source for information about the current disposition of firms, but in some cases this was supplemented with information from the *Wall Street Journal Index* (Dow Jones), various years.

Table 4-11. Average Number and Value of Acquisitions per Acquirer, 1955-89
Millions of 1987 dollars

Year	Number of acquisitions	Number of acquirers	Acquisitions per acquirer	Average value per acquirer
1955	114	92	1.239	183.643
1956	94	79	1.190	125.888
1957	75	69	1.087	78.379
1958	82	65	1.262	86.585
1959	132	99	1.333	96.709
1960	102	85	1.200	88.869
1961	113	90	1.256	156.823
1962	100	80	1.250	132.850
1963	121	98	1.235	133.932
1964	154	123	1.252	98.251
1965	166	118	1.407	123.560
1966	230	151	1.523	117.901
1967	352	200	1.760	177.822
1968	438	230	1.904	236.485
1969	427	234	1.825	179.619
1970	230	157	1.465	156.705
1971	178	118	1.508	100.289
1972	199	135	1.474	88.897
1973	168	132	1.273	88.326
1974	124	102	1.216	114.873
1975	99	88	1.125	80.189
1976	120	100	1.200	113.681
1977	162	143	1.133	111.775
1978	201	162	1.241	153.984
1979	442	365	1.211	140.792
1980	349	311	1.122	134.356
1981	533	437	1.220	179.654
1982	516	418	1.234	170.323
1983	529	441	1.200	146.835
1984	645	545	1.183	201.480
1985	745	608	1.225	186.394
1986	1097	839	1.308	194.116
1987	805	650	1.238	171.798
1988	614	528	1.163	275.601
1989	429	384	1.117	280.957

Table 4-12. Twenty-Five Most Active Acquirers, by Value of Acquisitions, 1955-78
Millions of 1987 dollars

Rank	Company	Number of acquisitions	Total value of acquisitions	Mean value
1	Atlantic Richfield Co.	9	10572	1175
2	International Telephone & Telegraph Corp. (a)	63	7402	117
3	Beatrice Foods Co. (b)	108	5084	47
4	Sun Co. Inc.	10	4217	422
5	Rapid American Corp. (c)	16	4134	258
6	Xerox Corp.	15	4057	270
7	City Investing Co. (d)	18	3974	221
8	Textron Inc.	30	3896	130
9	Gulf & Western Industries Inc. (e)	26	3761	145
10	Tenneco Corp. (f)	22	3653	166
11	Georgia-Pacific Corp.	43	3646	85
12	Inland Steel Co. (g)	4	3534	884
13	Monsanto Co.	7	3534	505
14	Mobil Corp.	6	3329	555
15	R.J. Reynolds Industries Inc. (h)	7	3182	455
16	Teledyne Inc.	42	3110	74
17	Lykes Corp. (i)	1	3081	3081
18	Sundstrand Corp.	7	3069	438
19	Warner-Lambert Co.	14	3051	218
20	Union Oil Co. Calif. (j)	7	2922	417
21	Singer Co. (k)	15	2802	187
22	American Brands Inc.	9	2798	311
23	White Consolidated Industries Inc. (l)	10	2680	268
24	Occidental Petroleum Corp.	12	2624	219
25	Kennecott Copper Corp.	4	2595	649

a) Now ITT Corp.
b) Subsequently Beatrice Cos. Inc.; taken private in LBO in 1986.
c) Now McCrory Parent Corp.; filed Chapter 11 bankruptcy in 1991.
d) Liquidated in 1984.
e) Now Paramount Communications Inc.
f) Now Tenneco Inc.
g) Now a subsidiary of Inland Steel Industries Inc.
h) Became RJR Nabisco Inc. in 1985; taken private in LBO in 1989.
i) Acquired by LTV Corp. in 1978.
j) Now Unocal Corp.
k) Taken private in LBO in 1988.
l) Acquired by AB Electrolux in 1986.

Table 4-13. Twenty-Five Most Active Acquirers, by Value of Acquisitions, 1979-89
Millions of 1987 dollars

Rank	Company	Number of acquisitions	Total value of acquisitions	Mean value
1	Philip Morris Cos Inc	3	18147	6049
2	Chevron Corp	2	17118	8559
3	Ford Motor Co.	16	14485	905
4	General Electric Co.	24	12936	539
5	Bristol-Myers Co. (a)	4	11907	2977
6	Texaco Inc.	2	11210	5605
7	USX Corp	4	11013	2753
8	Allied-Signal Inc.	10	11007	1101
9	Campeau Corp. (b)	2	9974	4987
10	E. I. du Pont de Nemours & Co.	7	9733	1390
11	General Motors Corp.	8	9262	1158
12	Mobil Corp.	6	9088	1515
13	Citicorp	10	8746	875
14	Beecham Group PLC	5	8049	1610
15	Dow Chemical Co.	9	7949	883
16	Occidental Petroleum Corp.	7	7071	1010
17	RJR Nabisco Inc. (c)	5	6477	1295
18	Bache Group Inc.	3	5756	1919
19	American Express Co.	14	5710	408
20	Shell Oil Co.	1	5578	5578
21	B.A.T. Industries PLC	3	5473	1824
22	Sony Corp.	4	5440	1360
23	Cooper Industries Inc.	12	5362	447
24	Eastman Kodak Co.	6	5346	891
25	Grand Metropolitan PLC	2	5343	2671

a) Now Bristol-Myers Squibb Co.
b) Two major department store subsidiaries filed Chapter 11 bankruptcy as of January 1990.
c) Taken private in leveraged buyout in 1989.

Active Divestors

Table 4-14 lists the twenty-five most active divesting companies, ranked by the total value (in constant 1987 dollars) of divestitures made from 1979 to 1989. Five of these active divesters were also among the most active acquirers during the same period, and seven had been among the most active acquirers of the earlier period. Five were foreign firms.

Source Notes, Table 4-14

In the data set covering 1979–89, divesting companies were identified by CUSIP number only, and divestitures were aggregated by CUSIP. The CUSIP Directory was used to identify company names associated with each CUSIP number. An effort was made to track CUSIP number changes for the large divestors. Because of restrictions imposed in defining the data set, divestitures by foreign companies include only those for which the acquiring company was based in the United States.

Table 4-14. Twenty-Five Most Active Divestors, by Value of Divestitures, 1979-89
Millions of 1987 dollars.

Rank	Company	Number of divestitures	Total value of divestitures	Average value of divestitures
1	General Electric Co.	17	5292	311
2	Tenneco Inc.	8	4941	618
3	RJR Nabisco Inc. (a)	8	4371	546
4	Campeau Corp. (b)	9	3963	440
5	Gulf & Western Inc. (c)	4	3520	880
6	Metromedia Inc. (d)	7	3496	499
7	RCA Corp. (e)	6	2661	444
8	AV Holdings Corp. (f)	3	2608	869
9	Union Carbide Corp.	5	2534	507
10	Grand Metropolitan PLC	4	2429	607
11	Beatrice Cos. Inc. (g)	10	2350	235
12	Unilever PLC	2	2002	1001
13	Goodyear Tire & Rubber Co.	5	1830	366
14	The British Petroleum Co. PLC	1	1800	1800
15	Esmark Inc. (h)	4	1790	448
16	Santa Fe Southern Pacific Corp. (i)	3	1750	583
17	General Cinema Corp.	2	1677	839
18	American Brands Inc.	5	1659	332
19	Dun & Bradstreet Corp.	3	1646	549
20	Occidental Petroleum Corp.	3	1581	527
21	Imasco Ltd	6	1538	256
22	Transamerica Corp.	6	1521	254
23	Gencorp Inc.	3	1508	503
24	The Singer Co. (j)	6	1493	249
25	Beneficial Corp.	3	1493	498

a) Taken private in leveraged buyout in 1989
b) Two major dept. store subsidiaries filed Chapter 11 bankruptcy in January 1990
c) Now Paramount Communications Inc.
d) Liquidated in 1986
e) Acquired by General Electric Corp. in 1986
f) Formerly Borg Warner Corp.
g) Taken private in LBO in 1986
h) Acquired by Beatrice Companies Inc. in 1984
i) Now Santa Fe Pacific Corp.
j) Taken private in leveraged buyout in 1988